Translation by **Anne-Claire Nivet**
Revision by **Susan Young**
Cover pictures: **Fabio Di Luca**

Preface

During the working season, customers sometimes ask me for recipes, which I always give gladly. However, some, including my employers, have urged me for quite some time to write an entire book.

'A book of my recipes?' I ask, astonished.

'But I'm not a chef!' I always reply.

I am simply a man passionate about cooking, someone who has gradually fallen in love with it, someone who has found it the most congenial way to express his creativity, emotions and passion. Someone who would basically live in a kitchen. One who was saved by cooking...

'Why should people care about my recipes?' I would ask. There are much better ones, in print and on the internet, and mine aren't necessarily original. They aren't even mine, after all. Recipes belong to everyone; recipes belong to those who make them. Sometimes I don't even have a recipe. I often cook by eye, I combine the ingredients intuitively, handfuls of this or that, here and there, a little more of this spice, a little less of that.

Nor am I precise or technical; I wasn't taught the techniques – I'm not professionally trained. I learned the techniques on my own, some I invented. I cook by instinct, sometimes I just cook according to the way I feel and the way I am. I mean, why would I want to write down recipes in a book? Why have them all lined up one after the other? Selected with what criterion? And what would be the point? What meaning would I give it?

For a few years I was facing a blank page, prey to small and large internal crises, because little by little the desire to write a book had settled inside me, but with little success.

Until one ordinary day, for no particular reason, I began to wonder when my culinary passion began, what the first thing was that I cooked, for example.

I started writing down old memories relating to cooking, the first things I saw, the first things I learned and... I couldn't stop! From the most distant internal image to the most recent experiences, the world of cooking has gradually illuminated my path and has given meaning to things and situations that I had not understood before. I was driven by a sudden urgency to clarify, to see in black and white the how and when of events, to unravel the intricate developments of a real inner transformation, thanks to the people and experiences that are now or have been in my life.

No, this is not an ordinary recipe book. I tried to write them down, but it really wasn't what I wanted to do. Then some images of my life began to appear in my head, together with some words, a perfume, a color; and then a specific pasta dish, a dessert that reminded me of a particular moment, a tasty bite that I had that very day...

No, this is not a book that aims to explain how to cook, because its purpose isn't to teach, rather, this book is the story of all those people and events that taught me something.

Enjoy your meal!

Sergio

Cooking
it's an honest statement
of who you really are.

You can't lie
in the middle of the fire
of passion.

You can only be.

Cook who you are.

A handful of gratitude

- I -

The most distant memory I have of cooking is a pan full of golden simmering oil and the hand of my grandpa guiding mine, teaching me how to immerse spoonfuls of dough, using caution and determination.

The image of me, just a few years old, standing on the chair in front of the stove, with the smell of the seaweed fritters filling the house of my paternal grandparents, will remain forever in my memories.

My grandfather was a chef on cruise ships, but also in his daily life. In the evening, his shift over, he enjoyed performing, accompanied by musicians, his repertoire of classic Neapolitan songs – at home, at family parties, private functions and local festivals. He also loved to write; often to his wife, his grandchildren, the people he loved. For me he was an example of a man from another era; who, contrary to the male archetype that prevailed at the time (especially in southern Italy), was always present in everyday life.

He enjoyed taking care of the kitchen, of the household chores, of the garden, of the pets, and of the love of his life, no longer independent in the last few years of her life. I remember the tenderness with which he combed her disheveled silver hair.

And the cuddles, the jokes, the kisses given unexpectedly, the hugs; after more than sixty years of marriage and a whole life together. Joyful, smiling and always ready with a joke.

Born in 1916, proud to be alive, from unknown parents whom he had always searched for, but without success, until 3 years before his death, through a heartfelt request on a television program dedicated to centenarians. He passed away a few years ago at the age of 103, having always lived in total autonomy.

The last time I was in Naples to visit him, I remember him shrunken and worn out, sitting on the armchair in the living room with a blanket over his legs and his eyes faded by the storms of an intense life.

'Sergio, I love you', were his last words to me. And the sea overflowed suddenly from my eyes hearing all the vulnerability he had never allowed himself to show before, and with that usual child-like tenderness, when they whisper it to you when they see you go away; which has the tone of a request, of a 'Stay with me' because you suddenly feel alone and defenseless.

While cooking, while singing, while writing, when I act silly at home to entertain my wife and children, I still feel the presence of my grandfather...

Frittelle di alghe

Ingredients for 4 people
200g of 00 wheat flour
12g of fresh brewer's yeast (half a cube)
50g of sea lettuce
approximately 150ml of sparkling water
salt and pepper
frying oil (peanut is recommended)

The first step in preparing seaweed fritters (*zeppole*) is making the batter. In a bowl sift the flour and gradually add 150ml of water in which you have dissolved the brewer's yeast.

Mix with a hand whisk to avoid lumps. The dough should be homogeneous and fluid, but not too liquid, like the consistency of a sticky custard. More water may be needed, depending on the flour absorption.

Let the batter rise, covered with a kitchen cloth or a lid, for about 1 hour, until it doubles in volume. Then add the chopped seaweed (washed and dried), a pinch of salt and a few grinds of black pepper and mix again to combine everything.

Heat the oil in a small, deep saucepan until it is slightly boiling. Using a spoon greased with oil (so it doesn't stick), fill it with batter and drop it in the oil, stirring gently. Fry 4 or 5 at a time.

The fritters should be slightly golden, but not too dark. Place them on absorbent paper to remove the excess oil.
Serve hot with a pinch of salt on the surface.

Note: It is not always possible to find sea lettuce. You can replace it with dried seaweed, for example wakame or dulse (just under half the weight) rehydrated in water for about fifteen minutes.

Variations: With this batter, it is possible to prepare different types of fritters. Substitute the seaweed with spinach and grated cheese, or with cauliflower tops blanched for 5 minutes, or with zucchini, zucchini flowers or sauteed peppers.

Risotto alla Pescatora

Ingredients for 4 people:
320g of carnaroli rice
1/2kg of clams
1kg of mussels
500g of squids
500g of prawns
4 red prawns
1 shallot
3 or 4 cloves of garlic
1/2 glass of dry white wine
1 bunch of parsley
Salt, white pepper and extra virgin olive oil

For the bisque:
1 carrot
1 stalk of celery
1 small golden onion
approximately 10 ice cubes
5 cherry tomatoes
1/2 glass of brandy

Arm yourself with patience. I recommend you start the preparations two hours before. Put on your favorite music. It's your moment of contemplation.

Start with the clams: submerge them for a couple hours in a bowl of cold water and 1 generous spoonful of salt to purge.

In the meantime, prepare the bisque: clean the prawns by removing the head, the shell and the tail, and put aside. Discard the eyes and intestines to avoid a bitter taste.. Cut the prawns into small pieces and store them in the refrigerator. Remove the shell from the 4 red prawns but leave the decorative head and tail.

Cut the carrot, celery and onion into pieces and fry them in a pan together with a crushed garlic clove and a few tablespoons of oil. After 5 or 6 minutes add the prawn shells and sauté them over high heat. Then add 1/2 glass of brandy, the chopped cherry tomatoes and a few stems of parsley and ice (the thermal shock will allow the shells to release their flavorful juices).

Cover all the ingredients with water and simmer for about 40 minutes. Then blend everything and filter the broth with the help of a fine mesh strainer.

Let's move on to the risotto: Clean the mussels by removing the byssus (or beard), pulling it down and rinse them by rubbing them together with your hands. Also add the drained clams and rinse.

Fry the mussels and the clams in a pan together with a few cloves of garlic, a sprig of parsley and plenty of crushed black pepper (you can also add some chili, if you would like).

Mix, put the lid on, and let them open for two minutes over high heat. strain the cooking juice and add it to the bisque: this will be the broth in which the rice will be cooked. Shell most of the mollusks, leaving some of the nicest ones aside for the plate decoration.

Cleaning the squids: remove the transparent bone found inside the squid and the guts. Remove the eyes and the teeth but save the tentacles. Rinse them and slice them into rings.

Finally, we can dedicate ourselves to the risotto: first heat the broth as it must be hot when you add it to the rice.

In a non-stick frying pan, fry a thinly sliced shallot in a few tablespoons of oil. When it starts to brown, add the rice and toast it for 1 minute over high heat, stirring continuously.

Deglaze with white wine and as soon as the alcohol has evaporated add the squid. Let it fry for another minute after which you can start pouring a couple of ladles of broth. Lower the flame and continue cooking for about 13 minutes, stirring occasionally. Add two more ladles of broth when the rice has absorbed almost all the liquid.

Add the prawns cut into pieces (in the meantime, you can sear the whole ones on a griddle or on a small non-stick pan with a spoonful of oil for a couple of minutes on each side, adding salt and pepper at the end).

Mix the risotto and then add the mussels and shelled clams a few minutes before it's ready. Taste the rice which should be 'al dente' and adjust the salt if necessary. Turn off the flame.

The consistency should be creamy but not too much (it will continue to dry even with the heat off). As my grandfather said, risotto must be like a wave: by giving the pan a sharp blow, the rice should fold back on itself, like a wave in the sea, precisely. If it's too dry, add half a ladle of broth and mix.
Finally, add some parsley and finely chopped garlic and stir.

Serve it very hot on a flat plate, giving it a few knocks underneath with the palm of your hand to spread it over the plate. Add one prawn per dish, a few mussel and clam shells, some more chopped parsley and white pepper.

Enjoy your meal. And may the sea be with you...

Torta Caprese

This dessert gets its name from the island of Capri, located in the Gulf of Naples, where it was created for the first time. Its story is handed down almost as if it were a legend, with different versions, but all agree on one thing: the praise of error. Due to forgetfulness or pressure due to the stress of the moment, the cook forgot to add the flour!

According to some, the first version of the cake dates back to the Bourbon era during the 18th century, when the Austrian Maria Carolina of Habsburg, wife of Ferdinand IV, nostalgic for her beloved Sacher cake, went into the kitchen to describe its flavor to the French chef, asking him to replicate it.

According to others, the current Caprese cake was born in 1920, by the pastry chef Carmine di Fiore, engaged in the creation of an almond and chocolate cake commissioned for the gangster Al Capone, who had come to the island for business. Distracted by emotion or by the fear of making a mistake, the famous pastry chef realized after baking the cake that he had forgotten to add the flour to the final dough!

The result was a dessert that was crunchy on the outside but moist and soft on the inside, which melted in the mouth. A masterpiece that today is appreciated all over the world.

Ingredients for a 24 cm baking pan
200g of shelled almonds
200g of dark chocolate
160g of sugar
120g of butter
3 eggs
a pinch of salt
zest of an orange
2 tablespoons of Strega liqueur (or rum)
icing sugar for garnish

In a food processor, or a powerful blender, grind the almonds into flour. Set them aside. Melt the butter in a bain-marie together with the dark chocolate chopped into small pieces.

Separate the egg yolks from the whites and whip the latter together with 80g of sugar and a pinch of salt. Set aside.

Whip the egg yolks for a few minutes with 80g of sugar until the mixture is smooth and frothy. Add 2 tablespoons of Strega liqueur (or rum) and the finely grated orange zest. Mix in the melted chocolate and butter, using a whisk. Then, with a spatula, stir in the almond flour.

Finally, incorporate the whipped egg whites, again with a spatula. Add them gradually and incorporate them inside the dough with movements from bottom to top. The final mixture should be dense and quite foamy.

Traditionally a buttered aluminum pan with flared edges (as used for Neapolitan *pastiera*) is used. Or you can replace it with a 24 cm loose-bottomed cake tin. Pour the mixture and level it with a spatula.

Cook in a preheated oven at 170°C for 40 minutes (or fan oven at 160°C for the same time). When tested with a toothpick, the dough should be slightly moist, but not sticky.

Let it cool completely on the tray before transferring it onto a serving plate. Coat it with icing sugar. Pastry chefs usually use a cake doily and alternate icing sugar with bitter cocoa for an impressive presentation.

The caprese cake can be stored at room temperature, covered with aluminum foil, for 3 or 4 days. It can also be frozen.

Pollo alla cacciatora

Ingredients for 4 people:

8 pieces of free-range chicken
1 onion
1 stick of celery
1 carrot
1 clove of garlic
1 sprig of rosemary
2 sage leaves

1 bay leaf
1 teaspoon dried oregano
1 can of peeled tomatoes
½ glass of red wine
1 handful of pitted black olives
1 tablespoon chopped parsley
extra virgin olive oil

Pour the oil into a large saucepan and fry the chopped onion, carrot, garlic and celery over high heat, stirring often to prevent them from burning. Add a pinch of salt and pepper.

Then move them to the edges of the saucepan with a wooden spoon and add the chicken pieces and brown them the same way. Add some salt, then half a glass of red wine and continue over high heat until the alcohol has evaporated completely.
Then combine the peeled tomatoes, a small, chopped chili pepper, the oregano, rosemary, sage and bay leaf, half a glass of water and a pinch of salt.

Bring to the boil and then lower the heat to minimum, cover with a lid, slightly ajar, and cook for about 30 minutes. Then add the black olives and raise the heat for a few more minutes to thicken the sauce, if necessary. Turn off and sprinkle with chopped parsley. Add salt if needed and your *Pollo alla Cacciatora* is ready. Enjoy your meal!

Note: You can replace the chicken pieces with chicken breasts cut in small pieces and floured.

II

My mother taught me to eat well (among other things) because she is a very good cook. The sense of taste, the pleasure experienced by the taste buds, the comfort given to the soul. And to wake up with a delectable smell permeating the house, the enchantment of a Sunday morning ragù simmering, the *cuzzetiello* of bread from which I removed the crumb from the center to fill it with tomato sauce: delicious late morning aperitif.

Through my mother I experienced food as if it were a messenger of love. Cooking for those you love, with attention and devotion, is an implicit way to let them know that you love them - she is not a demonstrative person.

Now she cooks less, but always very well. Until a few years ago, family reunions were held, often and willingly, at my childhood home. She started days before with the preparations of the desserts, the shopping, the marinades, the dough rising. Grandmother, uncles, aunts, cousins and friends.

Tables for 20 people, with triple starter, two first courses, two second courses, various side dishes, two or three types of desserts, fresh and dried fruit, liqueurs, digestives and coffee; foam on the surface, as at a bar. A menu worthy of the best restaurants.

I began to try my hand with desserts. She had me beat eggs with a hand whisk, sift the flour, and add the sugar. A few years later, an electric mixer entered the kitchen and I had great fun whipping up the dough and drawing concentric spirals swallowed and spat out by the rotating whips of the mixer, depending on the inclination it made millions of circles and stormy seas and hilly landscapes...

And it splashed all the mixture on the kitchen tiles, on my mother's apron, on my face. I couldn't wait for the moment she poured the dough into the pan and put it in the oven, because then I could lick everything that was left in the bowl with my fingers.

A pleasure, a triumph of sweetness; for me at the time it was ecstasy, like never before.

Yet, when she became engaged to my father, she didn't even know how to cook two sunny-side-up eggs. Then she met my grandfather, she says. Due to a sense of inadequacy mixed with a hint of good-hearted competition, she quickly learned the art of preparing meals for her own family and for an entire army of relatives.

In her, perhaps, I saw for the first time what it is like to be determined and tenacious, to never give up in the face of failures, to always persist. Her expression serious, she sometimes moves about the house anxiously, distracted or nervous, as if to say: 'Now don't bother me, otherwise I'll go crazy!'.

Then, finally, she smiles. At the table, when she at last sat down, at the first hint of someone's smile, at the first sighs of culinary pleasure.

At the first 'That's good, Mum, thank you!'

Ragù napoletano

Neapolitan ragù is a ritual, rather than a recipe. A unique dish par excellence for a Sunday lunch.

Eduardo de Filippo describes it very well in his masterpiece comedy *Saturday, Sunday and Monday*, brought to the big screen by Lina Wertmüller, with a superb Sophia Loren. In a memorable scene she ends up arguing with some of the butcher's shop customers for the honor of the real ragù recipe.

Ingredients for 6 people:
2 yellow onions
1kg of beef stew (cut into large pieces)
6/8 tracchiulelle (pork ribs)
6 Neapolitan chops (rolls of beef slices – recipe below)
200g of chopped pork belly lard
½ glass of red wine
2 bottles of tomato puree (1.5lt)
salt and black pepper
extra virgin olive oil
a handful of basil leaves

Slice the onions finely and sauté them in a large pan with extra virgin olive oil. With a wooden spoon, move them to one side of the pan and add all the pieces of meat, searing them over high heat on all sides.

Add salt, pepper and the red wine. Then cover with the tomato puree plus a glass of water, add salt and cover with a lid, slightly ajar. Lower the heat to the lowest possible level, add the basil and continue cooking for at least three hours, stirring occasionally.

Yes, Neapolitan ragù must *pippiare* - simmer slowly - so that you can almost hear one bubble of tomato sauce popping after another. The slow and gentle cooking is the real secret for the flavors to be perfectly blended and for the meat to be very tender.

Pasta can be garnished with ragù: tradition stipulates that ziti (a sort of long macaroni, tubular in shape like large bucatini) are used, which are broken with the hands before putting them into boiling water. Or ragù can be used in lasagna, alternating it with layers of bechamel and mozzarella.

But it can also be eaten as a morning or afternoon snack, simply by pouring spoonfuls of steaming ragù onto soft slices of bread.

Note: Some variations add meat balls, ham, bacon cubes or cervellatine (typical Campania pork sausages, thinner and longer than the classic ones...) into the large pot.

Braciole Napoletane

Ingredients for 6 chops:
6 slices of beef
40g of pine nuts
40g of raisins
approximately 70g of grated pecorino romano
a small bunch of chopped parsley
3 cloves of minced garlic
extra virgin olive oil
salt and pepper

Place the slices of meat on a cutting board and beat them lightly with a meat pounder. Sprinkle them with salt and pepper and evenly distribute the pine nuts, the raisins, and the finely chopped garlic and parsley. Sprinkle with grated pecorino Romano, making sure to leave the upper edge of the slice free.

Starting from the bottom, close the slices by rolling them tightly and seal them with two or three toothpicks that pierce the meat from the upper edge to the opposite side. They can also be tied with kitchen twine, like a roast.

At this point they can be incorporated into the Neapolitan ragù (previous recipe) or into a simple tomato sauce, with sautéed onions and basil.

We also recommend here a slow and prolonged cooking, for at least 2 hours, otherwise, as the great Eduardo De Filippo said in his famous poem entitled *O rraù* (*The ragù*): '...It's only meat with 'pummarola!''.

Zeppole di S. Giuseppe

Every March 19th, the feast of St. Joseph, which later also became the day on which Father's Day is celebrated, our house has never missed the typical Neapolitan zeppole. Double celebrations, for both father and mother, Giuseppina.

The dough is a simple choux pastry (the one used for cream puffs) usually fried (or baked for a lighter version) filled with custard and, as the 'icing on the cake', a cherry in syrup on the top.

Choux pastry ingredients (about 10 zeppole):
120g of water
2 medium eggs
75g of 00 soft wheat flour
60g of butter
a pinch of salt

Filling ingredients:
250ml of whole milk
1 egg and 1 yolk
50g of sugar
seeds from half a vanilla pod
20g of 00 soft wheat flour
lemon peel

cherries in syrup
icing sugar for garnish
peanut oil for frying

Start with the custard, because it will have to cool down: heat the milk in a saucepan with the vanilla and lemon zest. It is not necessary for it to reach the boil, it just has to reach 60°C.

In another saucepan, beat the eggs with the sugar until you obtain a frothy mixture (about 5 minutes). Add the sifted flour and mix until it is smooth and creamy mixture.

Pour gradually, in three stages, the filtered boiling milk and mix vigorously with a whisk to avoid the formation of lumps. Transfer the saucepan to the heat and continue stirring over low heat until the cream has thickened.

Transfer to a bowl and leave it covered with cling film until it cools down. To cool it quickly you can place the bowl in a larger container filled with water and ice.

Let's prepare the choux pastry: place the water and the butter cut into pieces in a saucepan and let it melt over moderate heat. When it is completely melted and begins to boil, add the flour at once, a pinch of salt and mix quickly with a wooden spoon. Once the mixture has thickened, continue cooking until the mixture comes away from the sides of the saucepan.

Transfer to a bowl and leave it to cool down for about 10 minutes.

Separately, beat the eggs with a whisk and gradually add them to the warm mixture, mixing quickly with a wooden spoon. It should be a smooth and dense mixture. Lumps may form initially. Don't be discouraged, keep mixing until you get the right consistency.

Place the choux pastry in a piping bag fitted with a large star nozzle and pre-heat the oven to 205°C (or 195°C in fan mode).

To form the zeppole you will have to make two circles with the piping bag, one on top of the other, in order to create a double circle, with a diameter of approximately 10cm, the center is left empty.

Cook for 20 minutes on the medium-low shelf of the oven, until they are golden. Leave them in the oven turned off with the door half open for another 10 minutes, so that they dry inside too.

You can also fry them a few at a time, turning them from time to time until they are golden. Then let them drain on absorbent paper.

When the zeppole are cold you can proceed with the filling. Fill the piping bag (the same one you used for the choux, washed and dried) with the custard and fill the zeppole one by one with a light pressure, then place a black cherry in the center and sprinkle with icing sugar.

The zeppole are ready! They can be stored in the fridge for a few days.

Pasta alla genovese

Contrary to its name, pasta alla Genovese is a typical Neapolitan dish and well known throughout Campania (and very little known outside the region). A Sunday dish par excellence, like the Neapolitan ragù, it consists of a creamy sauce of onions (lots of them) and beef, used to garnish the pasta. Usually hand-broken ziti are used, but I recommend trying it with rigatoni.

Ingredients:
320g of rigatoni
1kg of copper onions from Montoro (province of Avellino) or yellow onions
600g of lean beef (sirloin, rump)
100g of pecorino cheese
1 carrot
1 stick of celery
1 teaspoon of tomato paste
2 tablespoons chopped parsley
salt and pepper
150ml of dry white wine (a scant glass)
2 bay leaves
extra virgin olive oil

Fry the carrot and celery cut into small cubes in a pan with a few tablespoons of extra virgin olive oil. When they have browned, add the beef cut into cubes of about 4cm. Brown the meat well on all sides, then add a few pinches of salt and grated black pepper.

Add the finely chopped onions and sauté them over high heat for a few minutes. Add the bay leaves, a spoonful of tomato concentrate and half a glass of white wine.

Once the alcohol has evaporated, add another pinch of salt, the remaining white wine and cook on very low heat for about 3 hours, covered but not closed, stirring occasionally, and adding a few spoonfuls of hot water if it dries out.

At the end of cooking, there should be a brown creamy sauce, in which the pieces of meat will have fallen apart and mixed with the onions. Add the chopped parsley at the end of cooking and add salt if necessary.
Drain the pasta al dente and pour it into the pan with the still boiling ragù. To obtain an almost velvety creaminess, you can add a few ladles of cooking water. Its starch content will help to further thicken the meat and onion sauce.
Sprinkle with grated pecorino and...enjoy your meal!

Note: A less demanding and lighter variation is the version with tuna (preferably fillets in oil in a glass jar) with the addition of a few black olives and capers. Cooking times are halved, and the tuna should only be added at the end.

Babà napoletano

This dessert was born in the 18th century in Luneville, a small French town on the border with Germany, where the Polish king Stanislaus Lesczynski was in exile. He was a lover of the *kugelhupf*, a typical Polish dessert made with very fine flour, butter, sugar, eggs and raisins, but even though brewer's yeast was added to the recipe to obtain a soft and spongy dough, he still found it too dry.

After another unsuccessful attempt, losing patience, Stanislaus threw the dessert across the table, where it hit a bottle of rum, which began to soak into the dessert. And the greedy king, tasting it, was enraptured. A passionate reader of *One Thousand and One Nights*, he named his new dessert after his beloved protagonist: Ali Baba.

Subsequently, thanks to King Stanislaus' daughter Maria (wife of Louis XV and queen of France) and her pastry chef, Nicolas Stroher, Babà became the specialty of the Parisian pastry shop on Rue Montorgueil.

In 1800, the chefs of the Bourbon court were sent to France to learn the refined techniques of local cuisine, and returned to Naples with an enriched gastronomic knowledge, having learnt the techniques of the most famous dishes in Paris, such as the surtout which became the sartù of rice, the gateaux transformed into gatò of potatoes and the Babà, identical in name but with some modifications in the leavening (longer) and in the so-called 'bagna', lighter.

'Si proprio nu' babbà' has become a real saying in Naples, said above all of a person with a sweet and helpful character. A symbol of Naples, together with pizza and coffee, it is now in all respects a very common dessert, with a perfectly balanced consistency between creamy and impalpable, soaked in rum and sometimes filled with custard, cream or Nutella.

But the Babà that my mother makes is better than that of any pastry shop ;-)
This is the recipe:

Ingredients:
300g of 00 strong wheat flour (such as Manitoba)
4 eggs
100g of soft butter
20g of sugar
10g of salt
20g of fresh brewer's yeast (or a level spoon of dry brewer's yeast)
1 teaspoon vanilla powder

For the syrup:
500ml of water
250ml dark rum
180g of sugar
peeled zest of 1 lemon

10 single-portion molds

Work the eggs, sugar, chopped soft butter and brewer's yeast with an electric whisk for about 5 minutes (add a spoonful of water if you use dry yeast). Transfer to an electric mixer and add the sifted flour and salt. Work the dough until it begins to detach from the bowl. It will be sticky, this is normal.

Let it rest in the mixer for 1 hour, with a lid placed on top. Then knead for another 10 minutes, until the dough is firm. You can test its elasticity by spreading it with two hands to obtain the "windows effect".

Wet your hands slightly, take the dough with your hand, squeezing it between the thumb and the forefinger to pinch off pieces (like mozzarella), forming a ball which is placed inside the single-portion mold, previously buttered. It should be filled halfway. For an 8cm diameter mold there are approximately 65g of dough.

Cover the filled molds with cling film and place them in the oven to rise, with the door ajar and the light on for about 2 hours: they should almost triple in volume. Remove the cling film when the dough rises to the top of the mold.

Cook the babas at 180°C for about 22/25 minutes until entirely golden.

In the meantime, prepare the syrup: heat the water with the sugar and the lemon zest for about 5 minutes, stirring with a whisk to dissolve the sugar (it must not boil but it should remain at a temperature of around 60°C). Then add the rum, let it cool completely and remove the lemon peel.

Once the babas have cooled, they should be soaked in the syrup for about 5 minutes and then left to drain. If they still seem a little dry, repeat the operation several times.

My mother used to get up during the night to soak the babas. :-)
Let them rest for at least 3 hours in the fridge before serving.

III

Francesca is the one who gave me my first real cooking lessons, starting from basics: sautéed vegetables, sauces, béchamel sauce, custard, handmade pasta and the doughs of the great leavened products of the Neapolitan tradition.

Her childhood mentor had been her maternal grandmother, of the same name. A sweet elderly lady, tiny and friendly, with whom I spent days and nights, especially close to the holidays, preparing *casatiello*, *pastiere*, rustic and sweet cakes, *spaghetti alla chitarra*, lasagna, ravioli.

Even when we were engaged Francesca liked to cook for me the things she loved most when I was a guest at her parents' house, and her mother often instructed her to prepare more elaborate things when there were guests. Elaborate in terms of patience and precision. Her thoughtful and loving manners literally won me over from the starters! Breaded and fried anchovies, roasted peppers sautéed in a pan with olives and capers, mushrooms sautéed with carrots and courgettes, the *filoscio* (a thin omelette with a stringy heart of mozzarella or provola).

And she also makes the best tiramisu in the world. Many people tell her this; in fact, they often say it to me; I take compliments that should be hers because I'm usually the one who shows off, who passes off some of her delicacies as my recipes, but really - as we say – there's a great cook behind me.

Tiramisù di Francesca

Ingredients (for 1 tray of 6/8 portions):

1 pack of ladyfingers
250g of mascarpone
500ml of whole milk
90g of sugar
30g of 00 flour
3 eggs

3 cups of bitter espresso coffee
50ml of Marsala wine
½ vanilla pod
unsweetened cocoa powder
(for dusting)

The 'official' tiramisu recipe includes a cream of egg yolks and sugar whipped together and mixed with mascarpone (and sometimes cream).

In Francesca's recipe, the cream has been omitted and the eggs and sugar are whipped together with hot milk to obtain a custard.

Bring the milk almost to the boil in a saucepan, flavoring it with half a vanilla pod. In a bowl, beat the eggs with the sugar until they become light and creamy (about 4 or 5 minutes). Add the sifted flour and mix gently. Gradually add the hot milk, filtered to remove the vanilla pod, while still mixing.

Pour everything into a saucepan and let it thicken over low heat, stirring constantly. Let the cream cool down completely before mixing it with the mascarpone using a spatula.

At this point we can begin to assemble the tiramisu. Prepare two bowls large enough to dip the ladyfingers in: one with the coffee and the other one with the Marsala. Start by dunking the first layer of ladyfingers quickly in the coffee (2 seconds, no more). Arrange them on the bottom of the pan and cover them with about half of the cream. Proceed with a second layer, soaking the ladyfingers in Marsala (always for no more than 2 seconds, otherwise they might fall apart). Finish by spreading the remaining cream on the second layer and dusting with bitter cocoa.

Place it in the fridge for a whole night, at least. The longer we wait, the more the ingredients will be able to blend together or, as we say, make love together.

Parmigiana di melanzane

Ingredients for 4 people:
3 medium-large eggplants
750ml of tomato puree
3 eggs
150g of provola (or mozzarella mixed with smoked scamorza)
grated parmesan (8 or 9 tablespoons)
peanut oil for frying
a handful of basil leaves
1 clove of garlic
approximately 100g of 00 flour
extra virgin olive oil
salt and pepper

In a saucepan, fry a clove of garlic in a few tablespoons of extra virgin olive oil. Add the tomato puree and half the basil. Add salt and simmer for about 30 minutes, stirring occasionally.

Slice the eggplants thinly, a few millimeters thick, lengthwise and place them in a colander, lightly salting each layer and placing a weight on top: in this way they will lose part of their water. Leave for about 1 hour.
Cut the mozzarella into thin slices and let it drain in a colander.
Squeeze the eggplants, pat them dry with absorbent paper and fry them in boiling oil for a few minutes. Blot them again with absorbent paper. Prepare two soup plates: one with the flour and the other with the eggs beaten with a pinch of salt and pepper.
Dip the previously fried eggplants first in the flour and then in the egg and fry them again for a few minutes on each side.
In a baking pan, distribute a few spoonfuls of tomato on the bottom. Compose a

first layer of eggplant slices side by side, then spread the tomato sauce on top, sprinkle with the grated parmesan and distribute the provola (or mozzarella cut into slices) with a few basil leaves.

Continue in the same way with the subsequent layers (you should be able to do at least three). The last layer ends with the aubergines covered with a little tomato, a few slices of mozzarella here and there and a generous sprinkling of Parmigiano Reggiano.

Cook in the oven at 180°C for about 15 -20 minutes.
Excellent served hot or cold and it is even better on the following days.

Note: This is the original version of all Neapolitan housewives: the eggplants are fried twice. For lovers of strong emotions!

For a slightly lighter version you can skip the first phase of frying the eggplants and fry them only once, directly floured and dipped in beaten eggs.

IV

I started collecting cookbooks that came with some weekly newspapers for a small surcharge. And from them I began to experiment on my own. If there is a talent that I really recognize in myself, it is my ability to get inspired by recipes. I always read three different recipes for each new course I want to prepare, and then I do it my own way based on intuition, the desire to surprise, and the need to challenge myself.

At that time, this learning process was quite long: I had to read several books, some issued over a period of weeks, accumulating tons of magazines, and stealing ideas from the few cooking shows of that time.

Today, however, there are food bloggers, who with patience and meticulousness share their recipes, along with step-by-step photos, videos, tips and secrets.

I thank them every day, because with such an immediate and comprehensive access to the world of cooking, it allows many more people to experiment, to become passionate about this real and proper art. Even in moments of great pressure, when the mind struggles to remember a particular recipe or a step, just type key words on your phone and a world opens up.

Really, without the internet and the communication of food bloggers, the work of some chefs would not be the same.

My favorites? *Il Cucchiaio d'Argento, GialloZafferano, Misya, Tirmagno, Davide Zambelli, Ruben, Sonia Peronaci...* And then the chefs who inspire me most in some way: Pietro Leemann, Simone Rugiati and Antonino Cannavacciuolo.

Thank you to food bloggers, chefs, passionate cooks and influencers.
Sincere thanks. Thanks again today. _/_

Vellutata viola

Ingredients for 4 people:
700g of purple cabbage, washed
1 red onion
650ml of vegetable broth
a few grated nutmeg
2 cloves
2 grains of pimento (Jamaican pepper)
(the spices can be substituted by a teaspoon of allspice)
salt
extra virgin olive oil

To garnish:
1 or 2 tablespoons of sour cream (or kefir or Greek yogurt)
bread croutons
crispy bacon
seeds or dried fruit (pistachios, almonds, pumpkin seeds, sunflower seeds)

Slice the onion thinly and brown it in a pan with plenty of extra virgin olive oil. Cut the cabbage into thin slices and add it to a high-sided pan, browning it over high heat for about 5 minutes. Add some salt, the spices crushed in a mortar and cover everything with the broth. Cook over low heat, with a lid, for about 20 minutes, until it becomes soft.

Blend with a blender directly in the pan. Mix in cream and garnish to taste.

Note: Purple cabbage is among the most nutritious vegetables. Rich in minerals (such as calcium and iron) and vitamins. The sulphur content helps reduce cholesterol, glutamine helps relieve gastrointestinal inflammation and the antioxidants present, such as beta-carotene and lutein, prevent tissue ageing.

Cheesecake salata alla zucca

Ingredients for 6/8 portions:

4 packets of crackers (I usually use rosemary Tuc)
40g of melted butter
700g of pumpkin, peeled and de-seeded (I prefer Delica or Hokkaido for this recipe)
extra virgin olive oil
125g of gorgonzola
85g of robiola or mascarpone
1 egg
1 tablespoon breadcrumbs
salt and pepper
1 clove of garlic
nutmeg, cinnamon, chopped rosemary

To garnish:
Pumpkin seeds, a spoonful of grated pecorino cheese, a few spoonfuls of panko mixed with breadcrumbs and a sprinkling of sumac or smoked paprika.

Pulverize the crackers in a food processor and mix them in a bowl together with the butter. Butter a 20cm springform pan and distribute the mixture in the base, flattening it well with the back of a spoon. Let it rest in the fridge.

In the meantime, cut the pumpkin into pieces, season with oil, salt and pepper and cook it in a fan oven at 200°C for about 20 minutes. Keep aside about 200g of pumpkin cut into small cubes for the garnish.

Put the remaining pumpkin in a blender and blend it together with the garlic clove, egg, cheese, rosemary and spices. Pour the pumpkin cream over the cracker base, level with a spatula and garnish with the seeds, cheese, panko and sumac.

Cook at 170°C for about 30 minutes. Cover the surface with aluminum foil and continue cooking for another 15 minutes. Remove from the oven and let cool completely.

Can be served cold from the fridge or at room temperature.

V

I remember at the beginning, I used to make huge messes in the kitchen. My mother hated my culinary experimentation so much that one day she kicked me out of the kitchen and went on with her cooking...

Then little by little I started to cook something for Francesca and later on, with a little courage, also for my parents.

Love directed me towards the kitchen and cooking makes me feel love in return. And I truly mean it. I started cooking for love, to conquer, to speak through something I cooked, to which I have dedicated time and emotions.

Something I did just for you.

The first thing I cooked for Francesca? Stuffed mussels au gratin! I prepared them at my parents' house and I took them to her, still steaming, for lunch with her parents.

A success!

Cozze ripiene gratinate

Ingredients for 4 people:

1kg of mussels
200g of stale breadcrumbs
1 small fresh chili pepper
dry white wine (half a glass)
150ml cooking juice
50g of grated pecorino cheese
3 cloves of garlic
chopped parsley (two tablespoons)
pepper
breadcrumbs (2/3 tablespoons)
grated lemon zest
extra virgin olive oil (two tablespoons)

First, carefully clean the mussels, removing the byssus (or beard), pulling it towards the wider side of the mussel. Then rinse them and clean them under running water by rubbing them together.

Heat two tablespoons of extra virgin olive oil in a pan and fry a clove of garlic and a small chopped chili pepper for a few minutes. Add the mussels, add some ground black pepper and mix. Deglaze with the white wine over high heat and then place a lid on the pan. The mussels will open within one or two minutes. Turn off the heat and uncover to let them cool.

Strain the cooking juice and keep it aside. Soak the breadcrumbs in some of it.

Meanwhile, discard the empty half of the shell. Arrange the mussels lined up on one baking tray, covered with baking paper.

Turn on the oven at 250°C (grill function).

In a bowl, mix the squeezed breadcrumbs together with 1 clove of chopped garlic, parsley, cheese and grated lemon zest. The mixture should be moist but not wet. If too moist, add one or two tablespoons of breadcrumbs or, if too dry, add a few spoonfuls of cooking juice.

Using a spoon, fill the shells with the mussels one by one and sprinkle with a few more breadcrumbs on top.
Place the tray in the highest part of the oven and cook until the top becomes golden brown (about 3/5 minutes).

Serve them still steaming, at the house of the person you love!

VI

I moved to Rome three years before getting married, because of my insatiable desire to be elsewhere. I had obtained a surveyor's diploma but it wasn't really what I wanted to do in life; and the job market then, in Naples, was limited. And I, who felt like a stranger in my own land, needed to know if life was as I had been told or if instead there was something else; something that had a deeper meaning, something that was a real path, amongst those where you get lost and no longer know where to go.

It was necessary to distance myself not only from my family and my city, but especially from myself. From the image that I and those around me had of me. Because ultimately, everything that I knew about myself came only from other people's words...

At that time there was an explosion in the IT field and the main cities of the central and northern Italy were looking for professionals in this new field, which I had been studying for a year. Francesca joined me the following year (also working in that field). With our first savings we took a mortgage for a small house in the distant suburbs but close to the sea, and that was the temple in which I gave free rein to our common culinary passion.
'Love, I'll cook today, okay?'
'Okay, but as long as you let me cook something too...'.

We practically competed to see who could best grab the other by the throat, and not only that.
We learned to make love with ingredients. To balance the flavours, to enhance their taste, to preserve the colors, to stimulate the sense of smell, to ensure that the scents in the kitchen were an attraction for others who were in another room. What each of us prepared had to be able to seduce the other, to inebriate the senses.
To give pleasure. A pleasure that was totally satisfying (or almost).

Calamari ripieni in umido

Ingredients:
4 fairly large calamari
40ml of white wine
100g of chopped breadcrumbs
extra virgin olive oil
50g of pecorino Romano (optional)
2 tablespoons pitted and chopped black olives
2 tablespoons chopped parsley
2 cloves of minced garlic
salt and pepper

For the sauce:
1 clove of minced garlic
a handful of chopped capers
a handful of pitted black olives
750ml of tomato puree

49

Let's start by cleaning the squids: remove the transparent bone found inside the body and the entrails. Cut off the parts with the eyes and teeth but save the tentacles. Rinse them together with the body and keep it aside.

Chop the tentacles finely and fry them for two minutes together with two tablespoons of oil and the chopped garlic. Salt and pepper them, then blend them with the white wine. Turn off the heat and add the breadcrumbs to the pan (so that it absorbs the sauce). Add the olives, cheese, and the parsley. Mix everything together and if it is not very compact you can add a few spoonfuls of breadcrumbs; on the contrary, if it is too crumbly, add a few tablespoons of water.

Fill the squid pockets using a spoon, pressing lightly. Close the pocket with a toothpick.

In a pan, heat two tablespoons of oil with a chopped clove of garlic and cook the squid for no more than 5 minutes, over high heat, searing them on all sides. Add the capers, tomato puree and season with salt. Cook gently for about 30 minutes and add the olives a few minutes before cooking.

Note: To ensure that the squid is tender, not rubbery, you have the choice of two cooking times: 5 or 35 minutes. They don't like middle ground!

An alternative to stewing is to sear them in a pan or in a cast iron plate for just 5 minutes, but without continuing with the tomato puree etc.

You could season them with a citronette and plenty of chopped parsley, for example.

Gnocchi alla sorrentina

Ingredients for the gnocchi: (about 8 servings)
1kg of potatoes weighed with their skin
300g of 00 flour + 50g of flour for shaping
1 beaten egg
1 teaspoon of salt

Seasoning:
1 liter of tomato puree
300g smoked provola
(or buffalo mozzarella or fior di latte)
80g of grated parmesan
1 generous handful of basil

Gnocchi are one of the homemade preparations that Francesca and I make together (usually we divide the tasks).

Use old, floury potatoes because they are rich in starch, contain less water and will absorb less flour, so the gnocchi will be softer. The best are those with yellow flesh or with red skin (our favorites are those from Colfiorito).

The potatoes are usually put in cold water and boiled for about 30 minutes with the skin on. We, however, prefer steam cooking: peel them, cut them into pieces, salt them and steam them for about 45 minutes, or until they are soft when pricked with a fork.

Mash them with a potato masher while they are still hot and let the puree cool in a bowl for at least 10 minutes, until it is cool to the touch.

Season with salt and add the beaten egg and flour, kneading quickly, for just long enough to mix all the ingredients together (working the dough too much will

51

make it sticky).

Form a ball and cut the dough into pieces. Dust the work surface with a handful of flour or semolina. Make one-inch-thick loaves, dusting your hands with flour if they stick. Slice each loaf every 1.5/2 cm: the gnocchi are made ... but they are smooth. To create ridges, use a lightly floured fork and slide the dough along the inside of the fork, pressing lightly with your index finger; once the back has been scored, let it slide off gently (or alternatively use the special *rigagnocchi*).

As you make the gnocchi, you should place them on a lightly floured tray, spaced apart. Let them rest in the air for about 30 - 40 minutes so that they dry out slightly on the surface (so they won't stick to each other during cooking). However, do not leave them in the air for more than an hour otherwise a hard crust could begin to form.

In the meantime, you can prepare the tomato sauce: fry a clove of garlic in a pan with two or three tablespoons of extra virgin olive oil. When it has browned, remove it, lower the heat to minimum and pour in the tomato puree, the salt and lots of chopped basil, as if it were raining. Continue cooking for about 25 minutes, with the lid on. The sauce should be thick and full-bodied.

At this point you can move on to cooking the gnocchi. Cooking should be done in a large, spacious pan with plenty of water and coarse salt. You can tip the gnocchi directly from the tray, separating them if necessary. Turn them very few times during the cooking phase and do so delicately.

The potato gnocchi are ready as soon as they rise to the surface. Drain them with a slotted spoon and transfer them to a baking dish; add two or three ladles of tomato sauce and half the mozzarella and turn them gently. Sprinkle the surface with grated cheese, a few spoonfuls of tomato sauce scattered here and there and another handful of mozzarella.

Cook them in a preheated oven at 200°C with the grill on. Serve them hot and steaming.

Note: It is possible to freeze the gnocchi before cooking them: spread them well apart on lightly floured trays, suitable in size for your freezer.

Place them in the freezer and once they are well frozen you can transfer them into plastic food bags (to take up less space).

You can cook them in boiling water while still frozen (as indicated above); in this way they will retain the same softness and consistency.

VII

W e especially loved cooking fish-based dishes. We went early in the morning to the beach in Torvajanica, where the small fishing boats docked, and we stocked up on very affordable fresh fish, before it arrived in the shops.

We have never been very enthusiastic about dining out; we preferred inviting friends over for dinner rather than at a restaurant or some other places. And compliments for our synergy didn't take too long to arrive.

'But why don't you open a restaurant?' was asked more and more frequently. 'Why not?' ...one day this vague hypothesis popped into our heads.

But that's a whole other story...

Linguine alle vongole

Ingredients for 2 people:
500g of fresh clams
a dozen datterini or cherry tomatoes (red or yellow)
50g extra virgin olive oil
1 sprig of chopped parsley
1 clove of minced garlic
1 small chili chopped
salt and pepper
160g of linguine (or spaghetti)

First you need to purge the clams: eliminate the broken ones and those already open and pass them under running water, taking them few at a time in your hands, rubbing the shells together. Place them in a colander that you will then immerse in a larger bowl or pan filled with cold water and salt (20g of salt for each liter).

Mix with your hands so that the salt begins to dissolve.

Leave them to soak for a couple of hours, the minimum necessary for the clams to filter clean water.

Then drain them by simply removing the colander from the pan and rinse them under running water. The use of a colander prevents the clams from 'eating' the newly purged sand.

Pour the oil into a pan and brown the garlic for a few minutes. Add the chili pepper, the cherry tomatoes cut in half, a pinch of salt and some grated pepper. Add a few tablespoons of water and let them cook over high heat for about 7/8 minutes.

Then add the clams and leave them covered for about 3 minutes. Sprinkle with chopped parsley and turn off the heat.

Shell some of the clams if you prefer (it will be easier to stir the pasta).

In the meantime, cook the pasta in boiling salted water and drain it very al dente, 3 or 4 minutes before the end of the cooking time. Set aside half a cup of cooking water.

Transfer the pasta to the pan and stir on high heat for a few minutes. If the sauce is too dense, you can add a few tablespoons of cooking water.

Sprinkle with more chopped parsley and ...enjoy your meal!

Insalata di calamari

Ingredients for 4 people:
1kg of squid
2 carrots
2 zucchini
1 sprig of chopped parsley
1 whole clove of garlic
1 clove of minced garlic
1 lemon
salt and pepper
extra virgin olive oil

Cleaning the squids: remove the transparent bone found inside the body and the entrails. Cut away the eyes and teeth and save the tentacles. Rinse them under running water together with the bodies.

Heat the cast iron griddle and when it is hot, place the squid and cook them for a few minutes on each side. Salt and then let them cool.
With a very sharp knife, open the bodies lengthwise and cut them into strips (like julienne or spaghetti).

Fry a clove of garlic in a non-stick pan together with a few tablespoons of olive oil. Add the tentacles and cook for 4 or 5 minutes. Keep them aside.

Wash and dry the carrots and zucchini and cut them into julienne strips. In the same pan as the tentacles (they should have released some juice), fry the carrots over high heat for a couple of minutes, turning them often.

Add the zucchini, salt and pepper, and continue to cook for another 2 or 3 minutes, until the vegetables are well browned.

Combine them in a bowl together with the squid. Season with a drizzle of oil, garlic and chopped parsley and let them cool completely in the refrigerator.

When serving, add some lemon juice to taste.

VIII

After a few years in Rome we were able to realize all our dreams: an unforgettable wedding, a well-furnished house, a well-paid job, some new and good friends and ... the first child on the way!

In my seventh year as an IT specialist (and thanks to the imminent birth of our son) I officially entered a crisis. I didn't feel convinced that I could sustain myself much longer with that job.

We always had to keep up with new software and languages, but I had exhausted all my willingness to study those huge incomprehensible manuals or to take yet another refresher course. All of this just to continue working in a competitive and fast-evolving environment, which I couldn't keep up with any longer.

It was a crisis of work and social identity, which resulted, after a long period of incubation (and resistance), in real anxiety attacks. I felt the need to be a man with solid foundations, who could really count on his own resources. And perhaps I needed to present myself to my son with something concrete to pass on to him, something 'real' that I liked to do, that I was capable of making with my own hands.

Something that was creative...

Pizzette fritte (Neapolitan Montanare)

Ingredients for about 25 pieces

Dough:
350g of water at room temperature
12g of fresh brewer's yeast
or 1 teaspoon of dry brewer's yeast
300g of durum wheat flour
300g of reinforced flour (Manitoba type)
2 teaspoons of salt
10g of extra virgin olive oil

Seasoning:
1 clove of garlic
2 tablespoons of extra virgin olive oil
400g of chopped peeled tomatoes
or 400g of tomato pulp (one can)
1 teaspoon of salt
5/6 fresh basil leaves cut into pieces
1 tablespoon of dried oregano
50/70g of grated parmesan or pecorino Romano

Seasoning: Chop the garlic into small pieces and fry it for a few minutes in a saucepan with two tablespoons of hot oil.

Add the tomato, salt, oregano and basil and cook over low heat for about 25 minutes, with a lid placed (not closed) on top.

Dough: Dissolve the yeast in about half the water. Pour into the mixer or food processor and knead for about 5 minutes, gradually adding the flour and the remaining water.

Finally add the salt and a drizzle of extra virgin olive oil. Knead for a few more minutes until the dough is smooth and well combined. It should feel slightly sticky to the touch. Add more flour if necessary if it is too wet or a few tablespoons of water if it is too dry.

Grease a tall, narrow bowl with oil, place the dough shaped into a ball and let it rest, covered with a cloth, until it doubles in size (about two hours, depending on the room temperature).

The ideal temperature for the leavening to begin is around 24°. Usually, it is sufficient to put it to rise in the oven with the light on and the door ajar.

Take the dough and work it quickly on a work surface, using semolina flour on your hands if it sticks. Make balls of about 45-50 grams. Let them rise on the work surface, covered with cling film, for about 30 minutes. Then make discs of dough by flattening them with your fingers, starting from the center and widening them to the edges, taking care not to crush them too much. A rolling pin can also be used.

Let them rest for about 15 minutes.

In the meantime, heat the oil in a sauté pan and bring it to a temperature of around 180°C. Fry the pizzas a few at a time, turning them halfway through cooking until they are golden brown and puffy. Two or three minutes per side should be enough.

Place them on a tray with absorbent paper and salt them lightly. While still warm, put a spoonful of tomato in the center and some grated cheese on top. Serve them immediately.

Note: This is the classic version, but the pizzas can be topped in a thousand different ways. You can add anchovies to the tomato, or chili pepper. Or plain, or with a spoonful of burrata stracciatella and a very thin slice of mortadella, for example.
Be creative!

IX

It started with me leaving work at dusk and going into a pizzeria to get some practice.

We decided to take it over, I don't know if it was more from unconsciousness or from our need to get back into the game, now that we were a family and wanted to spend more time together, without delegating the upbringing of our child to someone else.

The first day I opened the shutter of our pizzeria I felt projected into a new dimension: finally mine!

I immediately felt at ease, even though there were things I had never done before: the orders, suppliers, preparations, the cash register, profits and liabilities, the relationship with the customers.

I felt that I was in a state of grace. Creativity began to flow not only for myself but for all those who wanted to try our unusual slices of pizza. Not only the classic and well-known flavors, but new combinations suggested by the seasons, vegetables grown nearby, the classic Italian first courses that I enjoyed converting into pizza toppings and any random clues that inspired me to invent new flavors: pizza with rocket, parmesan and strawberries, carbonara, al ragù, with wild boar sausage and berries, with melon, shrimp and liquorice, potatoes and lard, with mushrooms, truffles and chestnut compote...

It was a success in every sense. Thanks also to the support of our dear friend Anna, whom we met at that time and who remains to this day, in our feelings, a family member. A very good cook, practical and disciplined, she taught me, among other things, how to remain calm, to trust inspiration, not to fear bringing new ideas, so much that she would be able to put on a tray something I had just dreamed of.

A Neapolitan who makes Roman-style pizza in a pan, but with long leavening, with special flours and always new and well-found flavors. Word of mouth did the rest.

Our son arrived with Francesca in the late morning and the first piece of steaming white pizza was always his. He helped me restock the fridge in the afternoon, and late in the evening he fell asleep on the pizza boxes (on the large baking trays).

Was I a computer scientist? Suddenly I forgot even the simplest string of programming, as if I had always been a pizza chef and nothing else before. And I never wanted to do anything else in the world: I was in a full state of grace. What could have ever made me happier? Nothing!

Oh, no. In fact... yes!
'We are expecting a little girl.'

Maritozzi

The first version of the Maritozzi dates back to ancient Roman times, when wives used to prepare sweet loaves made with flour, butter, eggs and honey for their husbands, who went to the fields to work the land.

In the Middle Ages, a variant was enriched with nuts and raisins and apparently represented the only 'sin of gluttony' allowed during the Lenten season.

Between the end of the 19th century and the beginning of the 20th century, legend attributes to the name 'maritozzo' a playful deformation of the term 'husband'. In fact, it seems that this dessert was given by the fiancé to the future bride, as an auspicious gift, on the first Friday of March, corresponding to today's Valentine's Day.
Inside, embedded in the cream, there was often a hidden engagement ring.

Ingredients for approximately 12 pieces:
250ml of milk at room temperature
12g of fresh brewer's yeast (or a heaped teaspoon of dry yeast)
250g of 00 soft wheat flour
250g of strong flour (e.g. manitoba)
100g of sugar
2 eggs
80g of soft butter
zest of one lemon, grated
1 pinch of salt

For the filling:
500g of fresh whipped cream, without sugar
icing sugar to taste
1 egg
milk (a few tablespoons)

Dissolve the yeast in the milk in a mixing bowl. Add 250g of 00 flour, knead for a few minutes and let it rest for 30 minutes.

Then add the remaining flour, eggs, sugar, lemon zest and salt. Knead everything for about 5 minutes. Then add the butter, a small piece at a time, and continue kneading for a few more minutes, until the dough is smooth and elastic.

Form a ball, adding a little flour if it is too sticky, and let it rest in a bowl, covered with a cloth, for about two hours.

Divide the dough into balls of about 75g and stretch them slightly at the sides, so that they take on an almost oval shape.

Place them on a baking tray lined with baking paper and let them rise for another 40 minutes. Brush with milk and beaten egg and cook in a preheated oven at 170°C for about 20 minutes. Let them cool completely.

Cut the Maritozzi lengthwise (without cutting right through) and fill them with whipped cream. Use a spatula to level the surface and dust with icing sugar.

Eat them immediately or you can store them in a closed food bag, without filling them, for two or three days. If you can resist...

Pomodori ripieni di riso

Ingredients for 4 people:
8 tomatoes (marmande variety)
180g of rice (parboiled or currant)
5 potatoes
1 small bunch of basil
1 tablespoon dried oregano
1 clove of minced garlic
extra virgin olive oil
salt and pepper

Wash the tomatoes and cut the first upper slice for each one, which will be used as a 'lid'. Scoop out the flesh of the tomatoes and blend it. Then, in a bowl, mix together the tomato pulp with the salt and pepper, oregano and chopped basil.

Add the rice to the bowl and leave to macerate for at least an hour.

Then fill the tomatoes with the rice filling and close with the 'lid'.

This is the classic filling of the Roman recipe. You can enrich it to your liking with parmesan, for example, or mozzarella, olives and capers, or anchovies.

Arrange the tomatoes in a baking pan with the peeled potatoes around them, cut into chunks and flavored with salt, oil, pepper and chopped garlic (chili pepper is also excellent, if you prefer).

Sprinkle with salt and a drizzle of oil and cook in a preheated oven at 200°C for about 1 hour.

X

The transition from a 'good permanent job' to a small one as an artisan entrepreneur was not actually as sudden and instinctive as I described previously.

At first there was a large group of people (the people of Arkeon) with whom we shared our hardships and our goals in a circle, and then found ourselves unravelling again the tangled chains of our personal history, the archetypes of the Father and of the Mother, the wounds of our own inner child.

It was the beginning of a journey of exploration and discovery of that 'Sacred' part that 'pushes' each of us towards the realization of our own authenticity. A journey that was interrupted by the media pillory to which the association was subjected, due to accusations made by people in bad faith. The accusations were proven to be unfounded, but only too many years later.

Afterwards, a handful of psychotherapy sessions helped me discern the obses-sive thoughts of an imminent catastrophe that crowded my mind, from those – pure and legitimate – that dwelt at the bottom of my heart.

'You have to imagine yourself as the best pizza chef around, you have to visualize yourself preparing the best pizza in the country' the counselor advised me one day, while staring at a picture of a stormy sea posted in front of the bed on which I was lying, and all the fear of crossing the field of the known, which oppressed my chest, suddenly overflowed from my eyes.

A few years later someone actually complimented me, confessing to me that mine was the best pizza you could eat in the area, and then I remembered that little man in panic, crying on a counselor's couch, who was afraid to fail, to lose everything, to not be able to support his family anymore.

In truth, I fulfilled both 'prophecies'...

Carciofi alla romana

Ingredients for 4 people:
8 violet artichokes (or cimaroli)
4 cloves of minced garlic
1 bunch of Roman mint
a handful of chopped parsley
1 lemon
salt and pepper
extra virgin olive oil to taste

Let's start by cleaning the artichokes. Fill a bowl with water and lemon juice (this will help prevent the artichokes from blackening during the cleaning phase).

Arm yourself with disposable gloves, such as latex ones (to prevent your fingers from blackening too). Cut the artichoke stem to about 8cm and remove the hardest and most woody filaments with a peeler.

Remove the toughest leaves of the artichokes with your hands until they are softer to the touch and the base of the leaves is lighter. Cut the top part of the leaves to a couple of centimeters from the tip. Then, using a straight-bladed paring knife, cut slightly diagonally, starting from the base and moving upwards (where the hardest part of the leaves is located). Finally, gently open the leaves and remove the central beard with the help of a melon baller.

Dip them gradually into the lemony water as soon as you finish cleaning one. Mix together, in a bowl, the parsley and the chopped mint, garlic, salt, pepper and a few tablespoons of extra virgin olive oil. Season the inside of the artichokes, both in the center and between the leaves.

Then place them upside down in a pan with high edges and just enough width to contain them all (this way they won't fall to the side). Add a few more tablespoons of olive oil to the pan and begin to sauté over medium-high heat for a few minutes.

At this point add water to cover a little more than half of the head of the artichokes, and continue cooking over medium heat for about 20 minutes, placing baking paper or aluminum foil over the pan as a lid.

Before serving, turn up the heat to lightly sear them and make them crunchy.

Note: In the photo I had served them with a pecorino romano fondue flavored with gin: pour 100g of grated pecorino cheese, 125ml of cream and 25ml of gin, a few crushed juniper berries into a saucepan and cook over low heat for about 10 minutes, mixing with a whisk from time to time.

Cacio e pepe

The history of this dish has humble origins: it was born in the pastures of the Roman countryside, during transhumance. Shepherds used to fill their saddlebags with high-calorie, long-life foods, such as slices of pecorino cheese, dried spaghetti and peppercorns (which stimulate heat receptors and helped shepherds resist the cold).

Just three simple ingredients that gave life to one of the most representative dishes of Rome, as typical as the Colosseum, one could say. Precisely for this reason, for the dish to turn out well, it is necessary that these few ingredients are of excellent quality: the pecorino must be well aged but not too much (otherwise it is too strong); the ideal would be medium aging (18 months).

Black peppercorns are fine, but if you're looking for an excellent scent, I recommend Tasmanian peppercorns.

For the pasta, choose an artisanal, fresh one, made only with water and a good durum wheat flour (like Senatore Cappelli, for example, which is an ancient Italian wheat).

Ingredients for 4 people:
400g of pici senese (or tonnarelli or spaghetti alla guitar)
200g of grated pecorino romano
black peppercorns
salt

First, bring the water to a boil in a pan to cook the pasta. Don't add salt at this time. The pecorino romano is already quite salty on its own.

In a small bowl, mix the grated cheese and add a ladle of hot water (before it reaches the boil: the pecorino melts perfectly at around 55°C, beyond that it 'tears'). Mix with a spoon until you obtain a compact and grainy, non-liquid paste. The hot pasta will do the rest...

In the meantime, salt the cooking water slightly and begin to cook the pasta. Some don't salt it at all. I don't like the contrast between the savory cream cheese and the sweetish pasta. A little salt in the water makes the difference...

While the pasta is cooking, toast the crushed peppercorns in a pan, so that they can release all their aroma. Add a ladle of cooking water and simmer over high heat (you will obtain the so-called 'pepper broth' in which you will stir the pasta).

Drain the pasta very al dente (3 or 4 minutes before cooking) and reserve half a cup of the cooking water. Sauté it in the pan for two minutes to 'risotto' it: a technique used to prevent the waste of the starch that the pasta releases and add creaminess to the dish.

Turn off the heat and let it rest for a minute, so that its temperature is not too high when we mix it with the cheese.

Then add the cheese mixture and stir in the pasta using chef's tongs. Add a few more tablespoons of cooking water, if necessary, to achieve a smooth, creamy consistency. Serve immediately.

Note: In the photo I added some strips of fried speck. Sacrilege!

XI

An unprecedented economic crisis arrived in Italy (as always, between a government and the other): the one of the subprime mortgages, which broke out in America at the end of 2006 and arrived as a tsunami in many other parts of the world.

Many factories in the surrounding area closed overnight and customers dropped more than 30%. Our house, which we had mortgaged to take over the business, lost much of its initial value and we found ourselves paying a very high mortgage for a house that wasn't worth more than half of it. Taxes and additional costs did not drop by even a cent – on the contrary, the government was asking for further sacrifices for an economic maneuver defined as 'tears and blood' and I found myself spending, often alone, over 14 hours in just 30 square meters of...creative space.

In fact, when our daughter was born, Francesca, who had remained by my side, working practically until the day before the birth, had to step away from the pizzeria in order to look after our two children.

The distance from them was added to the burden of the debt collection companies that called one day and the following one too, along with our new and uncomfortable status of defaulters, especially towards the bank, which threatened to foreclose our house on the next unpaid due date.

'Since your wife left, your pizza isn't as good as it used to be' a client once confessed to me, on what I myself consider to be my 'day of truth'.

My hands were immersed in the dough, but my heart was elsewhere, staring at the family portrait on the screen of my mobile phone. I felt a deep sense of frustration for not being able to be with them, as I was forced to work harder to pay off the debts and to keep the business going. What was the purpose of waiting until ten in the evening, when I hadn't seen a shadow of a passerby for the last 3 hours? And oppressed by a system of bureaucracy and power that never changed, never showed any real interest in improving the quality of our lives and did nothing but let roll, grow bigger, the same problems as always on the backs of those who come after.

That exact day, like a ray of light through the narrowest darkness of my mind, from a place of silence rose unexpectedly and suddenly - almost by contrast – a feeling of burning love for my family. The tears were pouring down as I closed the shutter and got into the car to get back to them right away.

And that feeling of 'love is enough' spread all around.

I looked at the traffic and the people closed in their cars and I felt a sense of understanding for them.
The roots of pine trees splitting the asphalt, and they were so right. That pain of mine, that seems to start loving right here and right now. And the rain, with a thousand requests. And the wind, with its answers.

It was then that I began to understand that to be happy - and cook well - I had to follow my heart...

Tortino di miglio, zucca e zafferano

Ingredients for 4 people:
500g of cleaned pumpkin (for this recipe I used butternut or violina)
100g of hulled millet
200g of water
1 sachet of saffron powder (or a dozen pistils)
extra virgin olive oil
salt and pepper
2 cloves of minced garlic
breadcrumbs to taste
pumpkin and poppy seeds to taste
100g of grated pecorino cheese (optional)
butter to taste

Before being cooked, the millet should be rinsed several times under running water, through a sieve, until the water is clear. Then put it in a pan together with salted water (which must usually be double the volume of the millet), bring to the boil and continue cooking on a low heat until the water is absorbed (about 15/20 minutes).

Five minutes before the end, add the saffron: one sachet dissolved in half a glass of water; if you use pistils instead, calculate 3 or 4 per person and infuse them about half an hour beforehand, in a cup of hot water.

Cut the pumpkin into slices of about 1cm, season with salt, pepper, garlic and extra virgin olive oil.

Cook at 200°C for about 25 minutes. Then mash it with a fork and mix it together with the millet. You can add cheese if you prefer.

Transfer to a previously buttered baking tray and sprinkle with breadcrumbs, pumpkin and poppy seeds and chopped aromatic herbs if you prefer them.

Cook at 200°C fan oven for 20 minutes. You can serve it hot or warm.

XII

Over the course of the 15 years we lived in Rome - *caput mundi* - we went from feeling fully realized to completely destroyed.

We had to close the business, our house went up for auction and the job opportunities around weren't the best. But while many around us were sorry (rightly) for our failure, we started to look at events from another perspective.

'This apocalypse in our life seems to want to show us a new path' we said to console each other. And indeed, new changes in our consciousness and habits began to occupy a new space.

Our daughter, who refused to eat meat, gradually set us on the path of vegetarianism (and eventually veganism). One day, I put on her plate a little fried anchovy and she looked curiously at that little fish for a few moments. Then she took it slowly with her left hand and tore off a small crumb of bread with the right one. She brought it to its mouth, as if she wanted to feed it.

And the tenderness she showed at that moment opened the doors to a new world for us.

Flan di cavolo viola

Ingredients: (for 6 to 8 mini portions)
350g of already cleaned purple cabbage
1 red onion
150ml of fresh cream
2 eggs
60g of grana padano
2 cloves
3 or 4 grains of allspice
salt
extra virgin olive oil

For the fondue:
100ml of fresh cream
70g of Parmigiano Reggiano
pistachio grain to taste

For the cooking:
6/8 aluminum baking cups
butter to taste

Brown the thinly sliced red onion in a pan with a few tablespoons of extra virgin olive oil.

Slice the purple cabbage into thin strips and add it to the pan. Salt it, add the crushed cloves and allspice and as soon as it has wilted, pour in half a glass of water and continue cooking for about 15 minutes, over low heat and with a lid on. Turn off, remove the lid and leave it to cool down.

Transfer the cabbage into a blender and add the cream, parmesan and eggs. Blend until you obtain a thick and smooth mixture.

Butter the baking cups and fill them ¾ full with the mixture. Place them on a baking tray with high edges. Fill it with water so that the cups are immersed just over half.

Cook in a preheated fan oven at 170°C for 35 minutes. Remove the cups from the water and let them rest for 5 minutes before turning them over and serving them.

In the meantime, prepare the fondue: bring the fresh cream to the boil in a small saucepan. Turn off the heat and pour in the cheese, stirring quickly, until you obtain a velvety consistency. The more it cools, the creamier it becomes.

Pour one or two tablespoons of parmesan cream on each flan and garnish with chopped pistachios or whatever you prefer.

XIII

More time at home and more time together. When we managed to keep the worries about the future away, we felt like a lucky family, after all, because we had everything we needed. Everything that was important in life.

For a lunar year I tried growing vegetables, on a biodynamic farm not far from home. We always had good, fresh vegetables, therefore, cultivated by me.

Being around those 'solidarity purchasing' groups put us in contact with new people, some of whom later became dear friends. We bought products and organic raw materials locally and together we would meet at someone's house, taking turns to eat and cook, obviously, but also to share self-production knowledge.

Everyone brought something that they had prepared themselves and everyone shared their talent with the others. We felt like a small tribe.

We learned to make soaps, basic body care cosmetics, sourdough bread, and fermented vegetables. We collected the olives to make oil and fruit to make preserves. Sharing circles so as mutual support were present to nourish the soul.

All this, keeping ourselves busy with some home cooking and the various productions, was an emergency room for our mind, often crowded with obsessive worries which were not at all useful in solving our problems, but only in keeping us immersed in a state of precariousness, 'persecution' and injustice.

In this sense the kitchen saved me. When I cook it's just me, without anything else in mind other than the intent to create something appetizing; that is as good as a word of comfort and warm like a hug.

We met our friend Nicoletta almost by chance, and for fun we began to experiment together in some vegan and semi-raw food dinners at a cultural association. Both creative, we 'painted' dishes that had never been seen before with vegetables. The merchandising of the vegan world had not yet taken hold in Italy, and therefore it was difficult to find ingredients and products suitable for the purpose. That's how, gradually, partly out of necessity and partly out of desire, we learned to produce ourselves the basic foods of this new culinary world, such as seitan, tofu, cheeses, sauces.

The challenge at that time was to reinvent the great classics of the tradition in a plant-based version. In the shape, in the colors, in the flavors. A field known by few and in a short time I devoured entire books dedicated to the subject, from Shelton's hygienics to Ehret's 'mucusless diet'.

Then, almost for fun, I found myself sharing it with those requesting real cooking classes on how to make vegetable milks, seitan, and vegan desserts. Until I started as a personal chef at some dinners at private homes, an even more immersive experience in the relationship with customers.

The turbulence of recent times was undoubtedly accompanying us towards a new path.

Spaghetti di zucchine

con salsa all'avocado e pomodori secchi

Ingredients for 2 people:
2 medium-large fresh zucchini
1 avocado
1 small fresh spring onion
50g of dried tomatoes
basil to taste
1 tablespoon lemon juice
1 tablespoon apple or wine vinegar

The raw food diet is based on the consumption of foods (vegetable and others) that have not been exposed to temperatures higher than 45°C. Raw food is considered healthier and more nutritious than cooked food, because it does not lose enzymes, minerals and vitamins during the cooking process.

The first dish I learned to prepare was those very simple vegetable spaghetti, which I still eat now and then, as a substitute for pasta (but sautéed in a pan). You can also make spaghetti using eggplants, carrots, daikon, potatoes (then cooked in the oven) etc. and season them as if they were a pasta dish. It helps to trick the mind when you prefer not to eat cereals.

To make 'spaghetti' from zucchini, there are various tools on the market, ranging from a spiralizer to a simple serrated potato peeler.
In the absence of these you can use a very sharp knife and cut the zucchini into slices of about half a centimeter, lengthwise, and then each slice into julienne strips.

To eat raw zucchini with pleasure, I recommend choosing them very fresh, especially if they are large, because they tend to develop curcubitacin, a bitter and toxic substance, which could usually cause slight nausea.

If, like me, you don't like their raw flavor, you can sauté them in a pan with garlic and a drizzle of olive oil for a few minutes and then season them with the sauce.

If you don't like the crunchy texture of raw zucchini, you can place them in a colander and sprinkle them with a little salt, turning them occasionally. After an hour they will have lost part of their water and will have softened. You can squeeze them lightly and season them with the sauce.
Or you can marinate them, again for an hour, with salt, oil and lemon.

For the basic seasoning, which you can enrich with other ingredients, giving free rein to your imagination:

Soak the dried tomatoes in a cup of hot water and a spoonful of vinegar for about 30 minutes, then squeeze them. This way they will lose some of the salt used in the drying process.

Thinly slice the fresh spring onion. If you don't like its strong flavor, you can soak it in a cup of cold water and a spoonful of vinegar, then squeeze it. This operation will also make it more digestible.

At this point, place the peeled and pitted avocado in a blender, with a spoonful of lemon juice, the dried tomatoes, the spring onion and the basil. Blend until you obtain a creamy consistency; if necessary, add a few tablespoons of water.

At this point the sauce is ready and you can use it to season your ...zoodles!

'Veganduja'

Hopelessly addicted to the delicious Calabrian 'nduja (a sort of creamy, very tasty and spicy pork sausage), during my period as a raw vegan, I created a version suited to my dietary needs at the time.

I also partly used ingredients grown by myself and dried them (at 40°C in a dryer, about 14 hours for tomatoes and peppers, a little less for the other ingredients).

We all soon became addicted to it in the family, so much so that I prepared dozens of jars at a time. Little by little it conquered the palates of many friends and relatives too.

Ingredients for 2/3 jars:
250g of organic dried tomatoes
1 level tablespoon of dried chili
1 tablespoon of dried red pepper
1 clove dried garlic (or 1 teaspoon garlic powder)
1 generous grinding of pepper
a pinch of whole sea salt
1 teaspoon fennel seeds
1 teaspoon dried oregano
1 level teaspoon of smoked paprika
1 level teaspoon of Tabasco
1 heaped teaspoon of dried capers
approximately 200ml of excellent quality extra virgin olive oil

Simmer the dried tomatoes in 3 parts water and 1 part of white wine vinegar (used to desalinate them). Drain them, rinse them under running water and squeeze them lightly.

Leave them to dry overnight wrapped in a cotton cloth.

Place all the ingredients in a powerful mixer and begin blending at maximum power for about 30 seconds, gradually adding the extra virgin olive oil. Scrap the ingredients from the sides of the mixer bowl, if necessary. Blend for another 30 seconds and repeat the operation two or three more times, until you obtain a creamy and homogeneous mixture.

Pour into a glass jar and cover with more oil.

It can be kept for an infinite amount of time in the fridge (if you can resist) and because it is made with only dried ingredients, there is practically no risk of it going moldy.

Veganduja is excellent on croutons, to season pasta, or to flavor a soup.

Tartufini crudisti

If you need to avoid or limit your intake of sugar (and also of the fats often contained in desserts, especially industrial ones) these truffles are naturally sweetened because they use dates (but you can also choose another type of dried fruit, such as sultanas, plums, figs). The most valuable (and in my opinion also the best) variety of dates is the 'medjool'.

To sweeten them more you could also add half a ripe banana to the mixture.

Ingredients for about 20 truffles:
10 medjool dates
100g of dried nuts (hazelnuts, almonds, walnuts or even a mix of them)
25g of pumpkin or sunflower seeds
1 pinch of salt
1 or 2 heaped tablespoons of bitter cocoa (raw foodists use unroasted cocoa)

Soak the dates for about 15 minutes in a cup of hot water, so that they soften. Then pit them.

In a powerful mixer, put all the ingredients together until you obtain a homogeneous mixture that can be worked with your hands. If necessary, add a few spoons of the water used to soak the dates to make it softer. Or add a few extra teaspoons of cocoa to dry it out.

Let it sit in the fridge for an hour if you have trouble working with it. Take small portions of the dough, about the size of a walnut, shape into balls and store them in the fridge.

Being only dried ingredients, they can also be kept for 4 to 5 days.

What I propose is a basic version. But in reality, countless variations can be created.

You can roll the truffles in cocoa, coconut flour, chopped hazelnuts or pistachios... Place a toasted hazelnut or cherries in syrup in the center, for example. Add some coconut flour or even half an avocado and some melted dark chocolate to the dough. Flavor them with orange zest, vanilla, rum, or cinnamon.

In short, let your creativity flow!

XIV

As a spontaneous consequence, an ideal image of a different way of life made space within us, towards which we put our intentions, our energies, and our dreams.

Disillusioned and maladjusted, in an oppressive and unjust social system, we came across small communities of people, first virtually and then in person, who had chosen to abandon the comfort and inconveniences of a life that was too hectic and unaware, to live together in country houses or repopulate small semi-abandoned villages.

The common intent was to become as self-sufficient as possible, to no longer depend on the pressure and demands of a system that wants us to be perpetually productive, and which places God, instead of money, at the center of the universe, so as everyone's well-being, talents and right to happiness.

In those communities or eco-villages the days have a sustainable rhythm and are more on a human scale. We often share spaces for both private and working life, such as cultivation and production of food, craft works, construction of new living spaces, welcoming visitors, organizing the most diverse events, from those on personal growth to how to learn to weave chairs or other ancient crafts which are being lost. Some have even adopted an internal economic system, ranging from simple barter to the use of a complementary currency; oriented towards the use of renewable sources and methods of cultivation that are synergistic and more natural (even organic).

The world of cooking is therefore influenced by this lifestyle that is at the meeting point between the ancestral and something highly innovative, compared to what we are accustomed to living. The rediscovery of ancient legumes and cereals, of greens and other obscure vegetables that are equally valid from a nutritional point of view (but not very productive for the dominant economy system).

The children's school education is often organized on site through the establishment of parental or private schools, which usually choose more effective teaching systems, such as Montessori or Steiner, for example. And the decisions of collective interest are usually taken through assemblies structured in sharing circles that adopt the method of everyone's consensus. Everything turns on, at least in intentions, respect for people and the environment.

In short, a 'new little world' for all intents and purposes, where individual citizens become responsible, in a participatory manner, for what society (often Western) has marginalized, in favor of an endless race towards the self-destruction of the environment and the growth (the real, authentic) of people.

Orzotto alle ortiche

Among the pleasant discoveries of that time there were also wild herbs: dandelion, radish, borage, purslane, and nettles.

Plants that often have extraordinary properties and are richer in nutrients than cultivated ones. Nettles in particular are rich in calcium and potassium and have diuretic and anti-inflammatory properties. In spring the young stems and the more tender leaves are usually harvested, preferably wearing gloves because they sting.

In this recipe I use pearl barley but you can easily replace it with rice. Another discovery of that period, barley is in fact a cereal that pairs well with nettles, thanks to its anti-inflammatory properties for the gastro-intestinal and urinary systems.
Thanks to the beta-glucan content, it also slows down the absorption of carbohydrates, stabilizing blood sugar levels, and regular consumption helps keep the cholesterol levels at bay.

Ingredients for 4 people:
320g of pearl barley
500g of nettle leaves
1 fresh spring onion
1 liter of vegetable broth
½ glass of white wine
extra virgin olive oil to taste
150g of mature goat's or sheep's cheese
salt and pepper

Blanch the nettles in salted water for five minutes, then drain them and leave them immersed in water and ice for about 10 minutes. Then squeeze them and blend them in a blender until a paste-like consistency is obtained. Set aside.

Thinly slice the spring onion and sauté it in a sauté pan with a few swirls of extra virgin olive oil. Then add the pearl barley that you have previously rinsed and add salt and pepper. Stir to let the flavors mingle for a few minutes.

Add the white wine and when the smell of the alcohol has evaporated, add a few ladles of hot vegetable broth, stirring occasionally. Add a few more ladles of hot broth as it is absorbed, just as you would with a risotto.

About five minutes after the end of cooking, add the nettle cream and add salt if necessary.

Turn off the heat and let the barley rest, covered, for two minutes. Then add the grated cheese and stir gently.

Complete with a drizzle of extra virgin olive oil and serve immediately.

XV

We landed in the 'Green Heart' of Italy (in Umbria) thanks to an online announcement by a family that was looking for other people to collaborate on an eco-village project under construction.

Sharing living spaces (a large farmhouse on top of the hills) and work, both agricultural and for the management of the reception of pilgrims who traveled the 'The St. Francis way' and who stopped there for the night.

After some introductory visits we found ourselves, week after week - almost without realizing it – becoming an integral and enthusiastic part of the project, and within a month or so, we moved in permanently. Soon our little house in Rome would be auctioned off, and we preferred to leave it before being obliged to do so by some judicial officer. Still with the table set, with the coffee cups on the sink and the crumpled plaid on the sofa.

Like someone who had to run away, at the mercy of the Apocalypse...

Our children never knew (until last year) what had happened in detail. We prepared them for the idea of having to leave the house because of our desire to find a larger one, where everyone could have their own bedroom and with a garden large enough to grow vegetables and keep some farmyard animals.

'And will we sell the house?' they asked us then.

'No, because in reality it is not entirely ours. We will leave it to the poor. Those of the bank...'.

In the last moments we lived in Rome I remember that we often involved them in discussions like 'How do I imagine myself tomorrow, what would I like to do, where would I like to live....'.

'In the woods, mom and dad. We want a house in the woods!'

Pappardelle ai funghi porcini

Ingredients for 4 people:
400g of egg pappardelle
1 clove of garlic
300g of fresh porcini mushrooms (alternatively, frozen ones)
a knob of butter
½ glass of white wine
1 small bunch of chopped parsley
extra virgin olive oil
salt and pepper

Clean the mushrooms by removing the base of the stalk and the soiled parts and brush them with a damp cloth.

In the meantime, bring a pan of salted water to the boil.

In a sauté pan, sauté the crushed garlic clove in a couple of tablespoons of extra virgin olive oil. Remove the garlic and add the thinly sliced or diced mushrooms and let it brown on high heat for a couple of minutes.

Meanwhile, start cooking the pasta.
Blend the mushrooms with white wine and season with salt and ground pepper. When the wine has evaporated, add half a ladle of the pasta cooking water and leave to cook for another 3-4 minutes.

Drain the pappardelle al dente (always keep a cup of cooking water) and add them to the pan together with the mushrooms. Add the chopped parsley and, if necessary, a few more tablespoons of cooking water if the sauce becomes too dry. With the heat off, add a knob of butter, stir and serve immediately.

Penne alla Norcina

A simple and tasty dish typical of Umbria and more precisely of Norcia, due to the use of local ingredients in the preparation of this pasta which does not have an official recipe, but rather two totally different ones. Short or long pasta? Fresh cream or ricotta? Mushrooms or truffles?

However, both recipes agree on one thing: the use of Norcia sausage, characterized by its intense garlicky and tasty flavor.

Ingredients for 4 people:
320g of penne rigate
280g of fresh Norcia sausage
200ml of fresh cream
1/3 glass of white wine
100g of grated Norcia pecorino cheese
1 small black truffle (or two tablespoons of truffle sauce)
salt and pepper

Remove the skin of the sausage, crumble it using the tip of the knife (or simply breaking it up with your hands), and brown the sausage in a pan with a drizzle of extra virgin olive oil.

In the meantime, bring a pan of salted water to the boil.
Don't turn the sausage too often to help caramelize it a little. Add the white wine and when the smell of the alcohol has evaporated, add the fresh cream and bring it to the boil. Turn off the heat and add the truffle sauce (or half the grated truffle) and the cheese, mixing well.

Drain the pasta al dente and stir it in the sauce with the heat off for a few minutes.

Add some cooking water if it dries out too much (I imagine that at this point it will also have become your habit to keep half a cup of cooking water aside, right?)

Complete the dish with grated black pepper, a few flakes of cheese and slices of fresh truffle. Enjoy!

XVI

The experience with the pilgrims was absolutely enriching, on a human level and in emotional awareness. Each evening, we found ourselves eye to eye with new stories, different ways of living or interpreting life. And different ways of eating and being together.

We also organized different types of workshops and open days for everyone willing to know more about community life.

The time there was very extended and relaxing even though the work was intense: I spent the first part of the day in the synergistic garden. Then, depending on the season, we dedicated ourselves to the provision of firewood, to the preparation of the fields for the plantation of vines, and to the construction of a clay oven. Usually, Francesca or I were in charge of the lunch, always with great pleasure and always with some new recipes we wanted to try. Then we continued with lighter work and sharing circles, where everyone shared things like 'how am I doing, what are my needs, what do I want to do?'

In the evening we welcomed the pilgrims, who arrived from all over the world, tired and hungry, with many stories to share until late in the evening.

For a few months I felt I was daydreaming. I could no longer remember the pressure of having to go to work every day or the hours spent in the traffic. I just had to remember to live, as freely as possible, each new day rising like an enchantment from behind the Umbrian hills.

This experience ended within a year due to character incompatibility and differing points of views; and for the vital need to have some family privacy that nourishes us daily, in which we could always feel protected and welcomed, whatever happened. Where the role of parents and children was unequivocal, and where only one message could arrive loud and clear:

'We have everything because we have each other'.

Zuppa di porri e mandorle

Ingredients for 4 people:
4 leeks
150g of peeled almonds
2 tablespoons toasted unpeeled almonds
1 clove of minced garlic
extra virgin olive oil
saffron (1 sachet or about 15 pistils)
½ teaspoon of turmeric
salt and pepper

Soak the peeled almonds in water overnight.

Slice the leeks into thin slices and set aside a few handfuls of the green parts to be used for garnishing.

Brown the green slices that you kept aside in a pan with a few tablespoons of extra virgin olive oil, a pinch of salt and half a teaspoon of turmeric. First over high heat for a few minutes, then lower the heat and continue cooking for another 10 minutes or so, until they are crispy. Set aside.

Brown the chopped garlic and leeks in a pan with olive oil. Add the drained almonds, salt and pepper and cover with water to the depth of two fingers.
Let it cook over low heat for about 40 minutes.

Add the saffron pistils and blend everything until you obtain a velvety consistency. Season with salt and add a few tablespoons of water if it is too thick.
Garnish with crispy leeks and chopped toasted almonds.

XVII

Once again we had to 'smell' the events to understand in which direction the movements of our heart were blowing. We were more disillusioned than ever, because even our highest dream had been shattered: the dream of a different world, new, better!

A few months before the defeat, I had found a seasonal job at a vegan farm, not far from where we were.

Teresa, who ran the company together with her husband Aldo, was immediately enthusiastic about my creativity, my cuisine and my personality. She was the only one, at that time, who seemed to strongly believe in me, in a professional sense. A putative mother of a little man who was putting himself back into the world.

I started working alongside her in the kitchen to help her manage breakfasts, lunches and dinners for about twenty guests, who stayed for the whole week. The challenge for me was to learn to always come up with new menus, not to repeat the same dishes and to respect the guests' dietary needs.

She is a practical and effective woman, sometimes anxious but always lively and cheerful like a little girl. She flew around the stove and made sure everything had a good balance of flavor and texture. She wanted to taste everything before it was plated: she suddenly became serious, with pursed lips and wrinkled eyebrows. Then she looked me straight in the eyes and... blossomed into her best smile: 'But it's delicious!'.

Then one day, while she was welcoming customers into the room and inviting them to head to the buffet, she struck me by surprise:
'Now the chef will come here to present all these delicious things he has prepared for you.'
'Sergiooooo' she shouted towards the kitchen, inviting me to step into the room.

And, immediately blushing with embarrassment, I began my current habit of interacting with customers, presenting my dishes, telling a bit of their history and a bit of mine too.

Gradually, of course. Step by step. Deep inside I remain a shy man, even if 'exhibitionist'.

Panna cocco *(panna cotta vegan)*

Making vegan desserts was hell at first. The challenge for me was to replicate the flavors and textures of the traditional desserts that I loved most, without having to add too many refined or hydrogenated fats, or various thickeners.

Today I prefer butter to margarine or vegetable oils, and eggs instead of thickeners, coagulants, aggregators or too many insoluble fibers.

After a few attempts, I had to give up on some desserts. Cream puffs, for example. If you happen to have a healthy eggless beignet recipe, please let me know. For now it's an unsatisfied curiosity.

But I'm really proud of others. Like this panna cotta, for example.
Try it!

Ingredients for 4 single portions:
400ml tinned coconut milk
1 teaspoon of agar agar
15g of corn starch
50g of sugar
1 pinch of salt

Dissolve the cornstarch and agar agar in the coconut milk at room temperature. Add the sugar, a pinch of salt and bring to the boil, stirring occasionally, over moderate heat, for the mixture to become homogeneous.

Once it reaches the boil, continue stirring for about 2 minutes. Turn off the heat (it will still be quite liquid) and pour into single-portion molds.

Cover with cling film and let them cool to room temperature, then place them in the fridge for at least 6 hours.

When serving, detach the edges from the molds with a knife and invert onto the dessert plate.

You can dust it with cocoa and then coconut flakes, or pour on it a berry compote or a dark chocolate fondue, for example.

Risotto asparagi e fragole

Ingredients for 4 people:
320g of Carnaroli rice
1 shallot
1 clove of garlic
1 bunch of asparagus
250g of fresh strawberries
approximately 1 liter of already salted vegetable broth
½ glass of prosecco
salt and pepper
a spoonful of chopped thyme
60g of grated parmesan and a knob of butter
extra virgin olive oil

Wash the asparagus and dry them, then remove the hard part of the spears (I bend them one by one until they break on their own). Cut them into small pieces and keep the tips aside.

Wash the strawberries, remove the stalk and cut them into small cubes.

Slice the shallot thinly and sauté it in two or three tablespoons of extra virgin olive oil in a sauté pan. Add the chopped thyme, the pieces of asparagus, salt and pepper. Fry for a few minutes and then add the rice, toasting it for about a minute while stirring.

Pour in the prosecco and when the alcohol has evaporated, add ladles of hot broth until the rice is completely covered.

Cook gently and add a few more ladles of hot broth when the liquid is almost completely absorbed, leaving the risotto just barely covered.

After 5 minutes, add the diced strawberries, the asparagus tips and mix them with the sauce.

Turn off when it is al dente, making sure that the consistency is 'like a wave': by gently shaking the pan, the risotto 'moves' just like a sea wave.

Cover the pan and let it rest for two minutes. Uncover and stir in the parmesan and a knob of butter before serving.

Note: In the vegan alternative you can whisk with extra virgin olive oil and a mix of sesame, toasted and pulverized almonds, nutritional yeast and salt.

'Ricotta' di mandorle

Ingredients for 4 servings:
250g of peeled almonds
1250ml of water
50ml of lemon juice
1 teaspoon of salt

Required:
1 ricotta basket of 250g
a fine mesh strainer
a linen cloth

Soak the almonds in water overnight, then drain and rinse them. In a food processor or directly in a pan, with a blender, combine the water and almonds and blend until you obtain a smooth milk.

Turn on the flame and just before the liquid reaches the boil, turn off the flame.
Pour in the lemon juice, salt (you can also use a flavored salt of your choice), mix and leave to rest, with a closed lid, for 30 minutes.

Take a bowl (to contain the excess liquid) and place a fine-mesh strainer with a linen cloth on top of it. Pour in the almond curd to drain it and mix until a creamy mush is left inside the cloth. Close the cloth into a balloon and squeeze lightly to release additional liquid. Pour it into a basket and let it drain for about 3 hours, with a plate underneath, in the refrigerator.

Turn out and enjoy. You can season it with a drizzle of extra virgin olive oil and pepper.

XVIII

Aldo and Teresa are a close-knit couple who, in addition to being welcoming, are specialized in two very interesting fields.

He is a naturopath and enjoys, among other things, the cultivation of aloe vera from which he produces juices, cosmetics and macerates. He does iris reading and knows how to drag you into hypnotic shamanic journeys, accompanied by a hand-built drum.

She, as a counselor who can get straight to the point in five minutes, in the center of you, helps you release that emotion kept repressed for a long time and it is time now to let it overflow.

I grew up a lot with them, in many ways. The wounds of past failures slowly faded away, taking up less and less space in my emotional sphere and in me.
I began to have a minimum amount of confidence in myself, both as a man and as a cook.

The friendship and mutual trust were such that, the following year, they decided to entrust the management of the kitchen to me and Francesca. And it was crazy, extraordinary, an experience we will never forget! As a couple, as a family and above all as man and woman who put themselves to the test, after and despite everything, next to each other again in the kitchen.

I carry this in my heart: the time spent intensely together, the enthusiasm of the customers; the personal satisfaction of having managed to always overcome limited and stressful situations. And above all the help of various WWOFs (or workaways) who passed by to lend a hand (and more). We are still in contact with some, because even at distance, each travelling around the world, we remained dear friends.

What did I learn cooking with Teresa? Both she and Aldo are of Sicilian origin, so many good and tasty things, including: cassata, vegetable couscous and this aubergine caponata, for example.

Caponata di Melanzane

Ingredients for 4 people:
4 oval black eggplants
2 large red onions
4 or 5 celery sticks
1 tablespoon of tomato paste
1 clove of garlic
200g of copper tomatoes (or peeled tomatoes)
50g of desalted capers
150g of pitted green olives in brine
½ glass of white wine vinegar
a small bunch of basil
4 tablespoons of sugar
salt and pepper
extra virgin olive oil to taste

Wash and dry the eggplants, trim them and then cut them into 2.5cm cubes. Place them in a colander, with a plate underneath, sprinkling each layer with salt.

Place a small saucer with a weight on top (a pack of salt?) and let them drain for about 30 minutes. They will lose part of the water that is sometimes bitter and will absorb less oil during cooking.

Squeeze them a little at a time and fry them in a pan with plenty of oil until they are just golden.

Drain them with a slotted spoon and let them dry on absorbent paper.

Wash the tomatoes, remove the peel and cut them into cubes. In the same pan, fry the onions and celery, peeled and cut into slices.

Once browned, add the capers, tomato concentrate and olives. Brown for a few more minutes and then close with a lid, cooking over low heat for about 15 minutes.

Dissolve the sugar and vinegar in a glass. Then remove the lid and pour in the sugar and vinegar.

Stir until the smell of the vinegar has dissolved and add the previously fried eggplants, the chopped basil and mix well.
Add salt and pepper if necessary.

Let it rest in the fridge for at least 6 hours. It must be served cold.

Pasta alla Norma

Ingredients for 4 people:
320g of short pasta (paccheri in the photo)
2 or 3 long black eggplants
400g of peeled tomatoes
1 clove of minced garlic
a small bunch of basil
150g of salted ricotta
salt and pepper
extra virgin olive oil to taste

Wash and dry the eggplants, trim them and then cut them into 2.5cm cubes. Place them in a colander, with a plate underneath, sprinkling each layer with salt.

Place a small plate with a weight on top (a pack of salt?) and let them purge for about 30 minutes. They will lose part of the liquid, sometimes bitter, and will absorb less oil during cooking.

Squeeze them a little at a time and fry them in a pan with plenty of extra-virgin olive oil until they are golden.

Drain them with a slotted spoon and let them dry on absorbent paper.

In the same pan, with the filtered oil, lightly brown the chopped garlic, then pour in the peeled tomatoes, season with salt and pepper and cook for about 15 minutes on a moderate heat.

Add the eggplants and chopped basil and cook slowly for about another 5 minutes, stirring and combining the tomato sauce with the eggplants.

Cook the pasta al dente and add it to the Norma sauce.

Serve it by grating generous flakes of salted ricotta on each plate.

Cous Cous con *Ciambotta*

Ciambotta is a vegetable stew typical of southern Italy and each region has its own variant.

Ingredients for 4 people:

280g of durum wheat couscous
(not pre-cooked)
approximately 800ml of salted vegetable
broth
2 medium zucchini
1 yellow pepper
1 red pepper
2 long black eggplants
1 red onion from Tropea
500g of Pachino cherry tomatoes

6 potatoes
1 crushed garlic clove
salt and pepper
oregano
basil
parsley
½ glass of white wine
1 tablespoon apple cider vinegar
spicy paprika
icing sugar to taste

In 'our' Ciambotta the vegetables are browned in a pan and each flavored differently:

Eggplants: Wash them and cut them into cubes. Let them drain for about an hour in a colander, sprinkling each layer with a little bit of salt and adding a plate with a weight on top, to press them slightly. Then squeeze them and fry them in a fair amount of olive oil. Drain them on an absorbent paper and flavor them with pepper and dried oregano.

Zucchini: wash them, cut them into slices and brown them over high heat together with the thinly sliced onion. Add some white wine when they are golden, if you wish, and add a generous handful of chopped basil, salt and pepper. Turn off and keep aside in a bowl.

Peppers: Wash them and cut them into strips. Sauté them in a pan with a chopped clove of garlic and extra virgin olive oil, salt and pepper. When they start to brown, add half a glass of water and continue cooking, with a lid placed on top. When no more water is left, add a spoonful of apple cider vinegar over high heat for a few minutes. Turn off the heat, add some chopped parsley and combine with the other vegetables.

Potatoes: Wash and peel them and cut them into chunks. Fry them in plenty of olive oil until they are golden on all sides. Drain them on absorbent paper and add them to the other vegetables, mixing.

Cherry tomatoes: Wash them, cut them in half and place them in a pan with the cut facing upwards. Season with oil, salt, pepper, spicy paprika and dust with icing sugar. Cook in a fan oven at 200°C for 15 minutes. Add to the vegetables.

It is also excellent cold from the fridge, especially the following day.

Or as a condiment, in this case couscous: cover it with about half a liter of warm water and fluff it with a fork, then drain it (the water can be used to make broth). Bring a pot of vegetable broth to the boil and steam the couscous in the appropriate basket for about half an hour.

Place the couscous on a large plate, add salt and pepper and a few tablespoons of olive oil while fluffing it with a fork.

Add the ciambotta to the couscous and mix with a spoon to mix them together. Serve immediately.

XIX

When the following year Aldo and Teresa decided to retire, appointing a relative to manage everything, things suddenly changed again in our life.

The assumptions on which I had happily reinvented myself had disappeared, the methods and the different work objectives (no longer Francesca at my side) and also the motivations of my heart went to waste.

Francesca found a new job elsewhere and I decided to take a sabbatical year, during which I dedicated my body and soul to the care of our new house.

The Wheat House is a large, ancient farmhouse built in the 12th century on top of a hill; originally the watchtower of the Sorbello castle on the opposite hill, and later a grain-drying tower.

The farmhouse overlooks the border between Umbria and Tuscany, between the valley of Niccone and the valley of Pierle, between the castle of Reschio and the castle of Sorbello. Fully immersed in the woods, where wild boars and deer reign, in an absolutely wild and dreamy environment.

We rented part of it for just a few months, since the farmhouse wasn't equipped with a heating system and therefore was used only as a summer residence. But we immediately fell in love with it because, for the first time, even more than when we lived in Rome, it felt immediately like our true home.

Despite the inconveniences of an old farmhouse accessible only via a dirt road, with water that comes directly from a spring in the forest and single-pane windows that admit drafts and the small inhabitants of the microcosm, it was a refuge for us, after having just escaped in a messy way from the experience in the eco-village and with very little money in our pocket.

We later convinced the owner to rent it to us for a long period of time and we gradually readjusted it to our needs, buying a nice wood stove, cleaning up the surrounding vegetation and experimenting with some small works of maintenance and restoration which, little by little, transformed it into exactly that 'house in the woods' that we had visualized years earlier.

Lasagne alla bolognese

Ingredients for 4 people: 400g of
minced beef
200g of minced pork sausage
1 golden onion
1 stick of celery
1 carrot
1 clove of minced garlic
750g of tomato puree
½ glass of red wine
a small bunch of basil
salt and pepper
extra virgin olive oil to taste

Bechamel:
500ml of whole milk
50g of diced butter
50g of flour
salt, pepper and nutmeg

Required:
4 rectangular sheets of fresh lasagna
1 6-serving baking tin
2 mozzarella cut into cubes
6 tablespoons grated parmesan

First let's start with the ragù: fry the garlic in a sauté pan with the carrot, onion and celery cut into cubes (*brunoise*) with extra virgin olive oil. Add a pinch of salt and some black pepper.

As soon as they start to brown, move the sauce with a wooden spoon to the sides of the pan and caramelize the beef and pork over high heat. Add the salt and red wine. Mix the meat and the sauté vegetables together, and as soon as the smell of the alcohol is gone, add the tomato puree and the chopped basil leaves. Cook over very low heat, with a lid placed on top, for about an hour.

In the meantime, prepare the béchamel sauce. Melt the butter in a saucepan, then add all the flour and mix quickly with a whisk to avoid lumps. Slowly add the milk: cold, lukewarm or hot? I tried all three with identical results...

Mix over low heat until you obtain a homogeneous mixture. Add a level teaspoon of salt, a few grinds of pepper and nutmeg. Continue cooking, stirring constantly, until it is almost boiling.

At this point it should have thickened, but in our case the ideal consistency is slightly more liquid, like yogurt.

Spread a few spoonfuls on the bottom of the pan and we are ready to make the lasagna.

Place the first sheets of pasta on the layer of béchamel and spread a few spoonfuls of ragù on top of the pasta. Distribute a few cubes of mozzarella here and there and place the second sheet of pasta on top.

Spread a few spoonfuls of bechamel on it, plenty of mozzarella and a couple of spoons of grated parmesan. Lay down the third sheet and spread with more ragù and a few cubes of mozzarella.

Complete with the last sheet, mixing together the remaining bechamel with the ragù. Garnish with mozzarella cubes and grated parmesan.

Cook in a preheated oven at 180°C for about 25 minutes (the scent will let you know when it is ready). Let it rest for 5 minutes before cutting it.

XX

The house we currently live in is the place that returned us to having our 'feet on the ground'. I sank my roots in it and allowed my heart to blossom.

In parallel with the vicissitudes of work, we were able to draw on new internal resources thanks to a long process of 'reconstruction'. As a man and a woman, as a couple and as a family.

Thanks to the meeting with our dear friends Antonio and Simonetta (he a counselor of personal growth and a tantra master and she a counselor and pedagogist - among others skills they have acquired over the years) we had the opportunity to be helped through the use of techniques and tools that we did not know before: deep listening, the family constellations, the masculine and the feminine that is in each of us, a way of relating to others by focusing on one's own feelings, the release of judgement.

It helps you to look clearly and honestly at all the emotional baggage, made of old dynamics and past conditioning that we carry with us. And to recognize when we project them towards our partner, thinking that the other is responsible for our problems, when it is actually an ancient wound that begs to be heard, and often we can only see it if we project it outside of ourselves, in the attitudes of someone who, in that moment, acts as a mirror, as a messenger. As a Master.

In a society where more and more often love relationships break down at the first misunderstanding, celebrating 30 years of life together (and 20 of marriage) is for us a gift of inestimable value. And it is precisely the awareness that the origins of a conflict are shared equally between us that allows us to go further, certainly with no small amount of effort or pain.

But the first step is always to withdraw into oneself, to reconnect with one's deepest and truest part, to then be able to share a new part of the road together.

Choosing each other every time, trying to look in a direction that has common goals and dreams.

And entrusting ourselves, eye to eye, to that Sacred Spirit that lives inside us.

Brasato di bocconcini di cervo

I started eating game meat shortly after I arrived in Umbria. In the forest where we live, hunting is practiced periodically, and it happened sometimes that a group of hunters, to apologize for the disturbance caused to us during the year with the shots and shouts typical of wild boar hunting, gave us about 3kg of wild boar, already cleaned and cut into pieces, ready to be cooked or frozen.

Later on, I also visited the hunters' refuge (once harshly judged by my former vegan self) and had the opportunity to learn more about their customs and habits.

They meet periodically to clean and mature the animals, hold celebratory banquets and freeze their meat for consumption throughout the year. They prefer this meat to the traditional one, often coming from intensive farming, because it has a more intense and distinct flavor and is generally healthier and richer in properties.

My favorite today? Deer meat!

Ingredients for 4 people:
600g of venison meat
1 golden onion
1 stick of celery
1 carrot
1 star anise
2 crushed cloves
2 or 3 crushed juniper berries
2 tablespoons of tomato paste
extra virgin olive oil
salt and pepper

For the marinade:

Cut the meat into bite-sized pieces, place it in a container, add the vegetables cut into large pieces, the spices, the herbs and cover everything with red wine:

1 stick of celery
1 carrot
1lt of red wine (I used Ciliegiolo)
1 crushed garlic clove
2 crushed cloves
2 or 3 crushed juniper berries
2 bay leaves, 2 sprigs of rosemary, 4 or 5 sage leaves

Cover the container and leave to marinate in the refrigerator for 24 hours.

Remove the meat from the marinade and filter the wine. Bring it to the boil in a saucepan, add some star anise and let it simmer for about 5 minutes. Remove the star anise and set aside.

In a sauté pan, brown the carrot, celery and onion cut into small cubes in two or three tablespoons of extra virgin olive oil. Also add the pieces of meat and brown them over high heat until they are evenly browned. Add the spices, the bay leaf, season with salt and pepper and mix to make everything homogeneous, gradually pouring in the wine brought to the boil. Close with a lid placed on top and cook on the lowest flame possible for at least 2 hours.

The meat should be soft but shouldn't fall apart. If the wine sauce dries out too much, add some hot water and then add salt. The sauce should be thick and creamy.

In the photo I served it with fried polenta discs, boiled chestnuts, red currants and a sprinkling of pepper and parsley.

XXI

Covid arrived in the life of all of us just like lightning in a clear sky, at first accompanied by a sense of disbelief, then worry and frustration.

Once we got over the initial shock of that sudden upheaval in our daily habits, the quarantines represented for us a profound moment of reflection and retrospective of our life.

Having so much time for ourselves allowed us to focus on what really mattered to us, what was important to us as individuals and as a family. And we were able to see the fundamental need to have time for ourselves in order to clarify our minds, to recharge the batteries of dispersed energies in the frenzy of this time and to breathe a deeper sense of freedom, despite the constraints of the moment. The freedom to have your own mental and emotional time is best for our well-being.

In this sense, living in this uncontaminated and slightly out-of-the-world place has helped us immerse in an enchanted present, made up of long silent walks in the woods, shared activities inside and outside the home and a new charge of creativity that was able to express itself in multiple areas: from gardening to cooking, from writing to DIY.

The arrival of our neighbors, a little earlier, allowed us to share, in a more intimate and convivial way, much more free time together, compared to the rhythms we were used to before.

With Emma, a yoga teacher from London, we learned to dedicate an hour of every single day to physical activity, movement in general and meditative moments.

With Soudy, also from London but with Iranian origins, we exchanged flavors and feelings around our common passion: cooking. With her, an international cuisine cook (or ethnic), we were lucky to 'travel the world' through her dishes: Persian cuisine, Thai, and Indian. And English lessons in exchange for conversations in Italian, exchanges of opinion between different cultures and an always respectful and friendly neighborhood relationship.

Our best neighbors ever, absolutely!

Curry di ceci e spinaci

Ingredients for 4 people:
600g of pre-cooked chickpeas
2 red onions
400g of cleaned spinach
1 can coconut milk
2 cloves of minced garlic
1 fresh chili, chopped
1 tablespoon curry
1 sachet of saffron
1 tablespoon smoked paprika
2 tablespoons of tomato paste
2 tablespoons chopped coriander
extra virgin olive oil

Finely chop the onions and fry them in a sauté pan with a few tablespoons of extra virgin olive oil.

When they are golden, add the chopped garlic and chili, the cooked chickpeas, curry, tomato paste, salt and pepper.

Cook over medium heat for 5 or 6 minutes. Tip in the spinach and cook it for a few minutes until it is wilted.
Add the coconut milk and mix, bringing to the boil.

At this point, turn off the heat, add the saffron dissolved in a cup of water and the smoked paprika. Mix gently, cover, and let rest 5 minutes before serving.

Dahl di lenticchie

Ingredients for 4 people:
200g of hulled lentils
1 small onion
1 carrot
1 clove of minced garlic
approximately 750ml of already salted vegetable broth.
1 can coconut milk
½ hot chili pepper
extra virgin olive oil
1 teaspoon curry
½ teaspoon of turmeric
2 bay leaves
2 tablespoons of tomato paste

In a sauté pan, fry the thinly sliced onion and the diced carrot with 3 tablespoons of extra virgin olive oil.

Then add the chili and chopped garlic, the curry, the rinsed lentils and the tomato paste. Then salt and pepper. Then add the coconut milk and bay leaves and mix until smooth.

Cover by two fingers with vegetable broth and let it cook over low heat for about 25 minutes. Add a few more ladles of broth if it dries out too much.

The dahl should be thick but not too thick. At the end of cooking, add the turmeric, stirring, and a sprinkling of fresh chopped coriander before serving.

I often serve it with steamed or pan-fried basmati rice.

XXII

But who am I without my job? Which man do I see reflected in the mirror if I remove my social image? What would I like to continue doing and to what instead can I say NO to respect my Essence?

These and several others questions were the beginning of a true existential re-set, a new starting point from which visualize goals that could enrich me with new personal qualities, rather than a mere achievement of yet another goal, of a professional success, or of a more comfortable economic situation. Which today I clearly see as natural consequences of an incubation period spent overcoming internal obstacles, atavistic resistances, comfortable habits that we are afraid to let go.

I went through several different experiences at that time: from dishwasher to cleaning villas, from driver to assistant cook. In those places I had the chance to meet several people, including my friend Giovanni, a professional and enthusiastic Tuscan chef, who really loves what he does and knows how to pass it on to you. He's a true living encyclopedia of cuisine. He loves explaining the why and the how of the things he does, and he tells it to you while cooking ten thousand different things at the same time. Always good and characterized by that Mediterranean taste that takes me back home.

But the experience that helped the most to concentrate on the most appropriate methods to my desire of expressing myself in the kitchen, was that of a private chef in villas owned by foreigners, who returned to take refuge in the hills of Umbria especially in summer or during a few public holidays of the year. All thanks to Susan, my 'hook': one of the most honest, kind and precise New Zealand women I've ever met!

Lovers of Italian cuisine and eager to learn about the history and secrets of the most famous recipes, they opened the doors of their kitchen to me and, little by little, by winning their trust, they gave me the absolute freedom to do and decide.

Just like Robert and Elizabeth, for example, whom I literally adore! With them I could immerse myself, with great pleasure, in the daily life of their family, their culture, and their stories. Having the opportunity to interact with my clients so closely, having a way of knowing their habits and tastes, was a further source of inspiration, as well as a real recharge of energy, a renewed of self-confidence and a desire to get back into the game, to 'return to the world'.

And the Wheat House became quite naturally the theater of our best culinary performances and also the cradle of our most authentic desires, of our real basic needs. And the fertile soil from which our next new reality began to germinate.

Pappa al pomodoro con le vongole

One of the most representative dishes of Tuscany is certainly pappa al pomodoro, a poor dish dating back to peasant civilization and composed of tomato, oil, basil and stale bread. A recovery dish that releases tasty childhood memories.

My friend Giovanni taught me a very tasty version, made with the addition of anchovies, capers and chili pepper. From there it then came naturally to me to add something that also had the scent of a part of me, the scent of the sea...

Ingredients for 4 people:
700g of peeled tomatoes
300g of stale Tuscan bread cubes
2 cloves of minced garlic
1 fresh chili chopped
2 or 3 anchovies in oil
1 small bunch of basil
a handful of chopped parsley
extra virgin olive oil
salt and pepper
1kg of clams

First you need to purge the clams: eliminate the broken ones and those already open and pass them under running water and, taking them a little at a time in your hands, rub the shells together. Place them in a colander and immerse the latter in a larger bowl or pan filled with cold water and salt (20g of salt for each liter).

Mix with your hands so that the salt begins to dissolve. Leave them to soak for at least a couple of hours, for the clams to filter clean water.

In a sauté pan, fry the chopped garlic, anchovies and chili pepper together with 4 tablespoons of extra virgin olive oil for a few minutes. Then add the peeled tomatoes, a pinch of salt and pepper and the chopped basil. Cook very slowly for about 2 hours.

In the meantime, heat a clove of garlic in a pan with a drizzle of oil, add a handful of chopped parsley and the previously drained and rinsed clams. Close with a lid and leave to cook over high heat for 3 minutes. Turn off and let it cool down. Filter the cooking water and shell most of the clams (leaving some nicer shells for decoration).

Combine the broth with the shelled clams and the tomato, add salt if necessary and, with the heat off, stirring constantly, gradually add the bread cut into cubes. Stirring continuously allows the bread to soften until it falls apart, mixing in this way together with the tomato and clam sauce, creating a sort of mush.

Add a few ladles of hot water (or vegetable broth) if necessary if it is too dry.
Serve it decorated with some shelled clams.

Good either warm or cold from the fridge.

XXIII

Attention and care for my psychophysical well-being (the healthy habits learned during Covid periods) led me slowly to establish a less obsessive relationship with food. This has always been a blessing and a curse, as far as I am concerned.

Over the years I have experimented with different diets, motivated for physical reasons as well the need to remove from the act of eating all those emotional burdens that I had assigned to myself over time.

Eating to fill a void or to fill a need for pleasure and enjoyment that is never satisfied. Eating to feel loved and to experience a moment of comfort.

Eating compulsively out of frustration or stopping eating because I had enough of myself, of the world and of the thousand worries that boiled inside.

From an omnivorous diet I decided to move, in a single day, to the opposite extreme: the raw food diet.

Then came a period in where I followed a basically vegan diet; then a pescatarian diet, then periods without gluten or dairy products and others without sugars, alcohol or coffee. Up to a few days of total dry fasting or even for entire weeks in which I only drank centrifuged drinks. At first I felt better because I lost weight (any low-calorie diet makes us lose weight) but over time it has caused a significant dysbiosis and a visceral hypersensitivity.

Today I have understood that ultimately food is not my enemy, nor a partner on which to be emotionally dependent. No single food is the cause of my discomfort and completely excluding a category of foods, micro or macro nutrients, was like censoring something that was screaming in my gut; and not hearing it. Plus, for a long time, it was more comfortable for me to blame the food.

Now that I have returned to following a more balanced diet (at least I try) I look more honestly at my limits and the need for satisfaction (or compensation) that is hungrier in those periods in which (due to lack of time or too much mental stress) I fill my days with duties, with moments of little value, with trivial or frustrating things.

And I forget to 'feed' myself with quality time spent alone, where I can go back to what really makes me feel good, and that satisfies my need to feel what exists beyond the idea I have of myself, in the invisible that lives next to us every day, in the fascinating unknown that governs us.

Cavolo viola profumato al cumino
con carote glassate alla salsa tamari

Ingredients for 4 people:

½ purple cabbage
4 or 5 carrots
1 heaped tablespoon of cumin seeds
1 crushed garlic clove
½ glass of white wine

2 tablespoons toasted sesame
1 tablespoon chopped parsley
3 or 4 tablespoons tamari sauce
extra virgin olive oil
salt and pepper

Heat the cumin seeds in a pan with some olive oil for a couple of minutes. Slice the purple cabbage into thin strips and sauté it in a pan for about 7 or 8 minutes, stirring occasionally. Add salt and pepper and blend with the white wine. When the alcohol has evaporated, cover with a lid and continue the cooking for another 5 minutes over low heat. Keep aside.

In the same pan, add a few more spoons of olive oil, the garlic clove and let it brown over low heat.

In the meantime, using a potato peeler, cut the carrots into strips (like tagliatelle). Sauté them over high heat for about 5 minutes, taking care to turn them from time to time so they don't burn.

Pour in the tamari sauce, turn off the heat and mix.

In a serving dish, first place the purple cabbage and then the carrots. Sprinkle with toasted sesame seeds and chopped parsley.

XXIV

Being a chef today also means having to deal with dietary needs (often extravagant) of more and more people who, for personal reasons (I strongly advise not to, from repeated experience) or for health reasons, cannot eat this or do not prefer another.

If on one hand I see it as a challenge (my soul is always thirsty to test itself!) to develop inclusive and non-boring menus, on the other hand it gives me the opportunity to see more clearly all the parts of me that are still looking for compensation, the fears and judgments I had, and all that emotional burden related to what food represents for me, and that instead of 'censoring' I decided then to take with me to the kitchen.

Because deep down it still belongs to me; because in some way it is like an ally. Because it allows me to 'feel' my needs and those of others; because it provokes burning emotions in me, as if they were freshly 'cooked'. Which is basically anything that makes me feel alive every time. I really live, here and now.

In that search for a diet that 'makes me feel good', the danger is to lose touch with the feeling of gratitude we should feel for food each day. It is more and more taken for granted in our Western and 'advanced' society, full of shameful waste, while there are still people suffering from hunger. But a feeling that is necessary in order to heal that part of us that points the finger on the outside. That perhaps pushed the plate away with one hand and said, 'I'm not eating this' or 'this isn't good for me'.

But in truth, the food that reaches our tables is usually not poison.
Rather it is a gift. A gift from those who prepared it for us, a gift that we can give to ourselves. It is a gift that life gives us every day, because deep down nothing can be taken for granted anymore, in these times of great changes and environmental and climatic catastrophes.

A handful of gratitude can certainly be the secret ingredient that makes our dishes delicious, the ingredient with which we can enrich each of our courses so that it is truly nutritious and satisfying.

Gratitude for what I have now.
For who I am.
For what is in my life right here and now.

Risotto ai mirtilli, gorgonzola e noci

Ingredients for 4 people:

320g of Carnaroli rice
2 shallots
approximately 1 liter of vegetable broth
200g of fresh blueberries
+50g of fresh blueberries to decorate
4 tablespoons toasted and chopped walnuts
125g of spicy Gorgonzola
40g of grated parmesan
chopped fresh thyme
½ glass of white wine
extra virgin olive oil
salt and pepper

Thinly slice the shallots and sauté them in two or three tablespoons of extra virgin olive oil in a sauté pan.

Add the rice, toast it for about a minute while stirring.

Add the chopped thyme, salt and pepper and add the wine, stirring. When the alcohol has evaporated, add ladles of hot broth until the rice is completely covered.

Cook moderately and add a few more ladles of hot broth as the previous one is almost completely absorbed, leaving the risotto just barely covered.

With a blender, blend the blueberries together with the hot broth and add it to the risotto a few minutes after the end of cooking.

Turn off the rice when it is al dente, making sure that the consistency is 'wave-like': by gently shaking the pan, the risotto 'moves' like a sea wave does.

Cover the pan and let it rest for two minutes.

Uncover and mix first with the diced gorgonzola and then with the parmesan.

Decorate with fresh blueberries and toasted walnuts.

XXV

I had the pleasure of meeting Luca and Kriszti almost by chance, at the end of the first wave of the pandemic.

After a period of occasional collaboration, I was then hired as a chef at Terzo di Danciano, the 'Paradise on Earth' they manage and where I still work. Happily. And it is not just a way of saying...

Luca and Kriszti immediately gave me 'carte blanche', totally. Their continuous way of showing me their appreciation and enthusiasm for what I do is the primary source from which I 'feed' myself on a daily basis, from which I acquire further trust and personal satisfaction.

In addition to cooking, I am in charge of designing menus and shopping for primary materials, which allows me to see the ingredients with my own eyes and be able to buy them fresh daily.

We host groups (on average 15/20 people) from different parts of the world and who usually stay for a week. Yoga and dance students and teachers, mental coach, personal growth.

Every week we hold cooking classes and evenings where we all make pizza together, and day after day I can enter their world more closely, letting myself be inspired by what I perceive. Some come into the kitchen to exchange a few words, with others I stop to chat pleasantly in the room, and this possibility of interacting with such heterogeneous people, is absolutely enriching on both a human and a professional level.

Rather than preparing the same weekly menu for each group, I prefer to 'feel' what everyone passes on to me in a subtle way; and based on their needs and the type of seminar they do, I always try to make different things, drawing inspiration from the seasons and from what they transmit.

The enthusiasm and appreciation they show me in the evening give me the motivation to start again in the morning with new ideas, intuitions and real visions of the dishes that I want to prepare for the next day.

It is a 'dedicated' kitchen, precisely because I get to know the people for whom I cook and I have the opportunity to spend a lot of time with them during the week. Not only in the evening, when I show up with my playful English to introduce every course, but also during the day, when I happen to sneak in on some particular moment of the seminar and we find ourselves singing or dancing all together.

For them I'm usually the playful, histrionic cook who loves to entertain them during the week, not just at the table.

They are often an incentive for me to always do better, and with passion, the most beautiful job in the world.

Cinghiale in dolce-forte

An ancient recipe dating back to the Renaissance period, widespread especially in the area between Siena and Florence, *dolce-forte* is an accompanying sauce for stewed meat (particularly game). A mixture of dark chocolate, dried fruit, sugar and vinegar.

Strongly inspired by a recipe from *Science in the kitchen and the art of eating well*, by Pellegrino Artusi, a cooking manual from 1891, I was pleasantly surprised by the harmony of the flavors of this dish.
An experience to absolutely try at least once in your life.

Ingredients for 6 people:
1kg of lean wild boar
1 golden onion
1 stick of celery
1 carrot
2 crushed cloves
2 or 3 crushed juniper berries
extra virgin olive oil
salt and pepper

For the marinade:
Cut the meat into bite-sized pieces, place it in a container, add the vegetables cut into large pieces, the spices, the herbs and cover everything with red wine:

1 stick of celery
1 carrot
1lt of red wine (I used Sagrantino di Montefalco)
1 crushed garlic clove

2 crushed cloves
2 or three crushed juniper berries
2 bay leaves
2 sprigs of rosemary
4 or 5 sage leaves

Cover the container and leave to marinate in the refrigerator for 24 hours.

Remove the meat from the marinade and filter the wine. Bring it to the boil in a saucepan, and let it simmer for about 5 minutes for the alcohol to evaporate. Keep aside.

In a sauté pan, brown the carrot, celery and onion cut into small cubes in two or three tablespoons of extra virgin olive oil. Add the pieces of meat and brown them over high heat until they are evenly browned.

Add the spices, the bay leaf, season with salt and pepper and mix to make everything homogeneous, gradually pouring in the wine previously brought to the boil.

Place a lid on top and cook on the lowest heat possible for about 3 hours. The meat should be soft but not falling apart. If the wine sauce dries out too much, add some hot water (or vegetable broth) and then adjust the salt.

For the mixture:
3 tablespoons of pine nuts
1 tablespoon of honey
50g of dark chocolate flakes
3 tablespoons of raisins
1 tablespoon of candied lemon
1 tablespoon of ground cinnamon

1 teaspoon of grated nutmeg
100g of white wine vinegar
40g of sugar

In a glass, mix two parts of water with one of vinegar, sugar, cinnamon and nutmeg. Pour it at the end of cooking, stirring, together with all the other ingredients necessary for the mixture.

The sauce should be quite thick and enveloping.

Add some hot water (and possibly salt) if it is too sticky. Or cook for a few more minutes on high heat if it turns out too soupy.

Let it rest with the lid closed for an hour before serving (reheating it or even at room temperature).

XXVI

I want to confess a secret to you: I am, most of the time, never truly satisfied with what I do. This is my dilemma!

There is still a bit of a child's voice inside me who has learned from the world that you have to be perfect, impeccable, otherwise you will not be loved.

Here, to this day, through the most disparate experiences, I never reached that perfection. I want to learn to give it up.

And the warmth of the people who welcome me is a great, great help in this regard. Because you need to know that often, a minute before bringing the dishes to the table, I am convinced that I have cooked something bland or too savory, not cooked well, with a passable flavor. A minute later the enthusiasm of the guests proves me wrong and proves wrong the part of me that thinks that nothing I do is ever enough.

Just like Luca and Kristzi, who told me one day, when they saw me in the grip of sudden insecurities: 'You're not here because you always have to make amazing cuisine; you are here because we love you just the way you are!'.

Crumb cake ai mirtilli

Born after a series of not very convincing attempts, this dessert has now been at the top of the approval rankings of all the staff at Terzo di Danciano, including me.

Ingredients for a 20cm diameter baking pan (approximately 12 portions)

For the crumble:	For the filling:
400g of flour	500g of buffalo ricotta
130g of sugar	80g of sugar
1 teaspoon baking powder	
zest of 1 lemon	**For the blueberry sauce:**
100g of cold butter	300g of fresh blueberries
2 eggs	2 tablespoons of sugar
1 pinch of salt	

Cook the blueberries in a saucepan with the sugar and a spoonful of water over low heat for up to 5 minutes after reaching the boil. Let cool.

For the crumble, mix the dry ingredients so that they are homogeneous: the flour with the sugar, the yeast and the grated lemon zest.
Add the diced butter and the previously beaten eggs. Mix with your hands, pinching with your fingers, until you obtain a sandy and grainy consistency.

Butter the cake pan and pour half of the crumbly dough on the bottom, leveling with a spoon.

Mix the ricotta with the sugar vigorously with a whisk until you obtain a homogeneous creamy density. Pour into the cake pan and level with a spatula.

Do the same with the blueberry sauce and finish by sprinkling the crumble over the sauce until it is completely covered.

Cook in a preheated fan oven at 165°C for 40 minutes.

Leave to cool and serve dusted with icing sugar.

I advise you to taste it while still slightly warm, rather than cold from the fridge. It seems like a completely different dessert!

XXVII

Terzo di Danciano has become a second home for me, not only because I spend a lot of time there, but precisely because of this family and the friendly atmosphere that we breathe there. And the secret to every chef's well-being is to feel the esteem and the trust of the people for whom and with whom you work.

The entire staff is another essential foundation that allows me to be and to do what I want. Irony is our bread and butter and we are all moved by a great desire to do our job as well as possible, while having fun.

Especially with Anne Claire, the best assistant ever. French and a little American, or perhaps more a citizen of the world, in reality, because at the end of the season she leaves again and retraces the itineraries that reconnect her to her friends and family scattered everywhere.

Hers is a great job of support and patience because I'm not someone easy to keep up with. Usually, for example, we agree on the next day's evening menu, on who does what, on how to plate it, how to cook this or that ingredient. And then I arrive in the morning and maybe I've changed my mind, because someone or something inspired me differently or because I preferred to buy this ingredient instead of other. Or I get stubborn wanting to achieve something I can't do, or I complicate my day with last moment ideas. Modifying things that are perhaps already good and perfect just as they are. Maybe because, as she pointed out to me one day: 'It seems like you need to create a mess, to be creative. Maybe unconsciously....'.

And ultimately it is a sacrosanct truth that has characterized various moments of my life. If I look back - and this book is a precious opportunity to do so - I realize how much the moments of difficulty have allowed me more than anything else to express new potential, never known before. It is a more or less unconscious mechanism because I believe at the end that, to guide us along this 'learning path' that is life, there is something that pushes us in and drags us out at the same time, towards what awaits us. Some call it Spirit, some Collective Consciousness, some God.

Knowing this is perhaps not that important after all. What's important to me is to make it an experience.

Realizing, being aware of what happened to me and where I am now. Recognizing my share of responsibility. And recognizing that something magical happens to us every time, when we feel discouraged, lost, without a way out (because it happens to everyone, periodically).

Suddenly, after a lot of crying, the perception of what is now begins to become clearer, essential. Because it strips away all the mental construct that we carried around. And the soul, the life or who knows what puts us back on our feet, lights us up with renewed intentions. We have again the desire to try again, not to give up, to move forward.

It's the wonder, a miracle that happens every time, despite the disasters that occur in the world, the countless contradictions that make up life, with its outbursts of unmotivated joy and the inexplicable pain that afflicts us.

We perform this miracle every time we say YES again.

Pici al pesto di cavolo nero

(profumato all'arancia con pomodorini gialli)

Ingredients for 4 people:
400g of pici senese (or other fresh pasta without egg)
1 small bunch of kale
a handful of basil
40g of pine nuts
2 tablespoons of Tuscan pecorino
extra virgin olive oil
1 clove of minced garlic
peel of 1 orange
15 yellow cherry tomatoes
1 level tablespoon of icing sugar
salt and pepper

Wash the kale leaves and remove the toughest central rib.

Bring a pot of salted water to the boil and blanch the kale leaves for five minutes. Remove them with a slotted spoon (do not throw away the water) and leave them to cool in a container filled with water and ice (the rapid cooling helps to preserve the color of the vegetables and stop their cooking).

Cut the cherry tomatoes in two and season with salt, pepper, a drizzle of oil and place them on a baking tray lined with baking paper, with the cut side facing up. Dust with icing sugar and cook them at 180°C for 15 minutes in a fan oven. In the meantime, bring the water in which you blanched the cabbage back to the boil: we will cook the pasta in it.

Drain the cabbage leaves well and place them in a food processor together with the pine nuts, 7 tablespoons of extra virgin olive oil, basil, garlic, orange zest and pecorino.

Drain the pasta and season it in a bowl with the pesto. Add the freshly cooked cherry tomatoes and sprinkle with more grated pecorino, if you prefer. Enjoy!

Note: The best time to consume Tuscan cabbage is around January or February, or after the first winter frosts. Farmers in the area say that the leaves become more tender, less leathery and tastier.

Polpettine di salmone

Ingredients for 4 people:
500g of fresh salmon fillet
1 egg
about 3 tablespoons of breadcrumbs
1 lime (grated zest)
1 tablespoon chopped mint
1 tablespoon chopped parsley
1 mashed boiled potato
salt and pepper

For the sauce:
250g of Greek yogurt
1 small pre-cooked red beetroot
1 teaspoon mustard
1 clove of minced garlic
1 or 2 tablespoons of lime juice
1 tablespoon extra virgin olive oil
salt and pepper

Chop the salmon fillet with a knife and mix it in a bowl with the beaten egg, breadcrumbs, chopped mint leaves, lime zest, mashed potato, salt and pepper.

Use a spoon to take small portions of the dough and form the balls. Roll them in more breadcrumbs and fry them in extra virgin olive oil for a few minutes, until they are golden. For an optimal consistency I recommend forming the balls and letting them rest in the refrigerator for a couple of hours before frying them.

Once fried, place them to drain on a plate lined with absorbent paper and lightly salt them on the surface.

For the yogurt and beetroot sauce, simply blend all the ingredients together until you reach a creamy and smooth consistency. Add a few tablespoons of water if it is too thick.

Note: Passionate tip: Use wild salmon whenever possible.

The nutritional differences compared to the farmed one are notable. Farmed salmon is generally much fatter (even three times more) and calorific than wild salmon. Wild salmon, in addition to being richer in minerals, also has a higher concentration of collagen.

XXVIII

Yes, I'm happy. Insanely happy with the work I do and how I can do it. Not that I have an idea of what the future holds for me, but I am absolutely convinced that it is not the places that make the difference but the people you choose to surround yourself with. And how you allow yourself to be in their presence, if you give yourself permission to show up just as you are, by overcoming the fear of judgment (especially your own) and the fear of not pleasing, of not being loved.

This feeling of having the freedom to be who I am is ultimately what makes the difference for me. Since I have been here, in Danciano, I no longer have the feeling that I'm going to work, that I have to do this or that, by obligation. I'm going to be who I am, I'm going to do what I like doing.

Yes, I'm happy and I wouldn't want to be anywhere else doing what I do.

And I am immensely grateful.

I'm grateful to be able to do the job I love, with people I love, meeting so many nice people with whom I often stay in touch.

I'm grateful to have a beautiful family, a home and some good food. I am grateful to have Francesca by my side and that we are willing to travel together the wonderful adventure that is life. I'm grateful for everything that allowed me to be who I am today and to stay where I am now.

I am grateful because I can enjoy the warmth of the sun and the freshness of the rain. Grateful to still be able to be surprised by the small and large wonders of nature that surround us. To be able to become emotional, to be unafraid of what I feel.

And I'm grateful to be afraid because facing fear teaches me a new courage every time.

Pane Quotidiano

Making bread is one of the things I love most. I experience it as a mindfulness exercise, taking all the time I need, putting on calm music and almost contemplating every single phase of this miraculous process.

It starts the previous afternoon, with the refreshing of the sourdough, the gelatinization of the starches and the autolysis. I let the dough rest in the fridge all night; in this way I slow down the leavening process, favoring the maturation process (it helps the digestibility of the bread).

Then towards evening, the cooking, with its warm and enchanting aroma, which begins to spread everywhere. A cathartic moment that brings every inhabitant of the house near, one by one...

Use organic flours, because they do not contain glyphosate, a toxic herbicide.

This is the bread recipe we usually make at home:

Ingredients for a loaf of approximately 1.2 kg:
300g of durum wheat semolina flour (Senatore Cappelli variety)
300g of wholemeal flour (or a mix of them: wheat, spelt, rye)
350/400ml of water
150g of sourdough starter
20g of salt
10g of diastatic malt (optional)

Bring 60ml of water (80°C) almost to the boil, then turn off the heat and pour in 50g of semolina flour in one go, stirring quickly. You will obtain a sticky mass: let it cool completely (the so-called gelatinization of starches, which gives better structure to the bread and digestibility, thanks to the enzymes that break down the starch into sugars).

Knead roughly (by hand, if you wish) the remaining parts of the two flours and the water, for two minutes. It should not be a smooth dough but rather lumpy. Place it in an oiled bowl, covered with a cloth and leave it to autolyse for about 4 hours (it is a process which, among other things, helps the development of the gluten network).

In the mixer add the mother yeast, the diastatic malt (promotes and stabilizes leavening) and both doughs left to rest. Take small pieces at a time and add them gradually, kneading for about 4 or 5 minutes.
Finally add the salt and continue kneading for another 3 minutes.

At this point it should be fairly strung and smooth and slightly sticky (add more or less water until you reach this consistency).

Pour it into a large bowl, with a cloth placed on top and leave it to rest for 45 minutes.
Then, on a work surface, proceed with the folding, 3 times every 30 minutes: roll out the dough gently to form a rectangle. Lift one of the two longer sides and fold it towards the center. Lift the other side and fold it over the previous one.

Do the same with the two shorter sides: lift the first, folding it towards the center and then lift the other side, folding it over the previous one, making them fit together. Turn the dough over, squeeze it slightly into the shape of a ball, place it in the bowl and cover.
Let it rest for another hour.

Then transfer it to the work surface and shape your bread, dusting with more semolina flour. Place it in a proofing basket, cover it with a cotton cloth and place it in the fridge for 12 hours (or overnight).

The leavening and fermentation process will be slower and more controlled and the flour enzymes will have more time to split starches into sugars (maturation). This will give the bread a deeper, more aromatic flavor.

Preheat the oven to 210°C, with a saucepan of water inside.

Take the bread from the fridge, turn it upside down onto the baking tray and make cuts on the surface.

Then place the pan with the bread in the lower-middle part of the oven and cook for 45 minutes.

Remove the saucepan, lower the temperature to 190°C and cook for another 15 minutes, until the crust is golden and its scent has begun to permeate the room. Leave in the oven, turned off with the door ajar, for another 10 minutes. Place the loaf on a rack to cool, leaving it covered with a cotton cloth.

Slice, close your eyes and savor.

Yes, this state of immediate happiness and profound satisfaction has to do with gratitude...

The constant act of cooking
means committing
to put your heart
into something

Also today.

Index

Starters:

First dishes:

Second dishes:

Side dishes:

Desserts:

 **sergio.tancredi**

Made in the USA
Coppell, TX
02 November 2024

39523100R00107